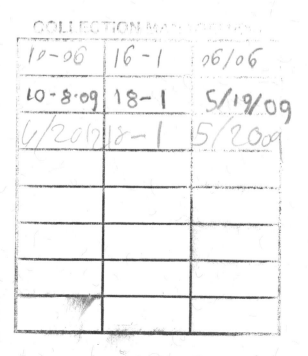

# HOW TO
# COLLECT
# DEBTS
# (AND STILL KEEP YOUR
# CUSTOMERS)

# COLLECT
# DEBTS
## AND STILL KEEP YOUR
# CUSTOMERS

# DAVID SHER AND MARTIN SHER

# AMACOM
## American Management Association
New York • Atlanta • Boston • Chicago • Kansas City • San Francisco • Washington, D.C.
Brussels • Mexico City • Tokyo • Toronto

This publication is designed to provide accurate and authoritative information in regard to the subject matter covered. It is sold with the understanding that the publisher is not engaged in rendering legal, accounting, or other professional service. If legal advice or other expert assistance is required, the services of a competent professional person should be sought.

Library of Congress Cataloging-in-Publication Data

Sher, David.
    How to collect debts (and still keep your customers) / David Sher and Martin Sher.
        p.   cm.
    Includes index.
    ISBN 0-8144-0487-1
    1. Collecting of accounts.   2. Debt.   3. Debtor and creditor.   I. Sher, Martin.   II. Title.
    HG3752.5.S53   1999
    658.8'8—dc21                                    99-19945
                                                        CIP

658.88

Printing number

10   9   8   7   6   5   4   3   2   1

This book is dedicated to **Morris Sher**, our father,
who taught us his core values.

- To be honest
- To treat all people with dignity and respect
- To continuously improve

# Contents

# Preface

## We Grew Up in Credit and Collections

Morris Sher, our father, grew up as one of seven children in Birmingham, Alabama, in the twenties and thirties. The population of Birmingham was generally poor, especially during the Depression, and our father's family was no exception. His father, Victor, was out of work much of the time and even moved to Arizona for a while because of his asthma. Dad wasn't the oldest child, but he assumed much of the financial responsibility for the family. At thirteen he got a paper route, getting up at 4 A.M. to deliver the morning edition before school and then delivering the afternoon edition after school. He did his homework after dinner and studied late into the night. He had a great work ethic and was conscientious and responsible. Even with all of his extra responsibilities, Dad graduated high school near the top of his class.

After high school, Dad worked as a traveling salesman, but he always had a desire to go into business for himself. The only problem was his lack of money. So how do you start a business from scratch with virtually no capital? He became a peddler where all he needed was a car and a willingness to work hard. He started out selling dresses to housewives by driving back and forth between customers and the wholesale district since he couldn't afford an inventory. He asked his customers for a 50-cent down payment and then collected 50 cents a week until the purchase was paid for. The wholesaler sold to Dad on credit and increased Dad's credit line as weekly payments were made.

Dad soon realized that his growth potential was limited to how many houses he could visit each week. It would be much more efficient to open a retail store and have his customers come to him. In 1938 he opened a small store and then married Sylvia, our Mom, the next year. With someone to watch the store, he could go out to collect payments and convince his customers to come to the store. His customer base grew not only because he could offer a bigger and better selection, but because he also offered the ease and availability of credit with a very small down payment.

When World War II broke out, Dad enlisted. He and Mom packed up, left the business to his father and brother to operate, and went off to war. When they returned in 1945, there was little business left to salvage and, for all practical purposes, they had to start over again. They persevered and opened a new, much larger store in 1948 under the name of the New York Clothing Company—The Home of King Kredit. Dad made a strategic decision that King Kredit was going to be the store with the easiest credit in town. Instead of having low prices and high credit standards, he figured if he got a down payment close to the cost of the merchandise, he could sell to everyone with little risk. King Kredit became the clothing store of choice for anyone with no or bad credit. Dad had large bad debts, but enough people paid to guarantee him a profit.

We entered the family business when we were about eight or nine years old at Dad's suggestion that it was time for us to help out. So while other boys were out with their friends playing baseball and football and having the times of their lives, we were taking credit applications and verifying them, asking for down payments, explaining our expectations of payment, and making collection calls. To say we grew up in credit and collections is an understatement. We learned the basics of accounts receivable management before we learned the multiplication tables.

## The Lessons of Life

Time marched on, Dad died suddenly, and we found ourselves with families of our own and a business that would have to grow in order to support both families. We decided to move to a larger location and sell furniture and appliances in addition to clothing. We made the move, changed the name to Mr. King Furniture, and spent money on remodeling, inventory, and advertising. Then we waited for the customers to line up.

We had, however, overlooked one small but significant detail. When we sold only clothing, the average shirt and pair of pants cost $15 or $20 and we collected a down payment that covered or came close to covering that cost. But when we asked our customers for a proportional down payment on a $400 or $500 purchase, the customers still had only $15 or $20 to pay down. Obviously, then, we didn't sell much furniture.

We had to reduce down payments to generate more sales. We rationalized that people would pay better for furniture and appliances than for clothing, and if they didn't, we could always repossess. With this new strategy, our sales volume did increase, but we ran into a new problem. Keep in mind that we were appealing to customers with the message, "If you have no credit or bad credit, we are here to help you." Our customers, of course, included those who had been turned away elsewhere as poor risks. So it shouldn't have been a shock to us when many of these customers didn't pay as agreed.

Up until now, we didn't have to be good collectors. Now we had to get serious about collections to survive. If we didn't do everything just right, we would be out of business. With our relatively small customer base, we knew we couldn't do hard-core collections or we'd run all our customers away. We had to find a way to collect that was persistent and consistent, yet still leave our customers feeling comfortable enough to come back and buy from us again.

We traveled all over the country talking to retailers in similar businesses. We joined every trade association that could help us with credit and collections. We talked to finance companies, credit jewelers, rent-to-own dealers, bankers, pawnshop owners—anyone who could teach us about credit and collections.

We discovered that one key element to success in the collection business is finding the right employees and getting them motivated and excited. We learned how to hire, train, motivate, and pay collectors. We hired a full-time programmer who designed all of our software from scratch because existing software was based on the premise that most people pay and only a small minority do not, and our situation was the exact opposite. We wrote everything into our computer system we could dream of and constantly made improvements based on our actual experiences. We even brought in a firm to develop a sophisticated credit-scoring system whereby we could ask a customer five simple questions to determine the odds of payment.

## A New Perspective

Finally it dawned on us that if we could collect Mr. King Furniture accounts, the collection of other people's accounts receivable would probably be easier. We had the people, systems, training, and technology in place, and so we started AmSher Collection Services. We began by doing collection work for other retail stores and then got referrals to collect for utilities, colleges, and government agencies. We got requests to collect for hospitals, medical clinics, and doctors' offices. Doctors and medical administrators appreciated that our collection systems were developed to collect money and still maintain the goodwill of their patients.

We then built a commercial collection department that specialized in business-to-business collections. We found that the same collection principles used for individual consumers were applicable to business collections. However, we did have to hire more sophisticated collectors knowledgeable about business laws and practices. In 1995 we incorporated a new business called AmSher Outsourcing for businesses strong in their specialties but weak when it comes to collections. We collect in the client's name so AmSher is invisible. We not only increase their cash flow, but save them money because we convert their collection department from a fixed to a variable expense.

Because we own and operate different credit and collection businesses, we have a unique perspective on collections and accounts receivable management. We view the collection process as business owners and not as bad debt collectors. We have had to hire collection agencies and collection attorneys for our retail accounts even though we own our own collection agency. Consequently, we have seen collections from both sides and gained valuable experience. We understand how to evaluate outside collection services and how to determine whether they're doing a good job.

## Sharing What We Learned

We have given numerous talks to businesses, medical practices, hospitals, and trade associations on accounts receivable management. We have evaluated accounts receivables for banks to evaluate loans and we have done all types of consulting and training. We know collections from beginning to end, and we've put what we know into this book.

People used to do business on a handshake. If they made a commitment to pay on a certain date, they honored their commitment. Now it's generally expected that payment be made slowly so cash can be held longer. The world is changing and will continue to change. You need to understand these changes and adjust how you run your business and your collection strategies accordingly.

When you finish reading *How to Collect Debts (and Still Keep Your Customers)*, you will have a broad and deep understanding of the collection process that will help you adjust. If you follow the principles we present, you will increase your sales, maximize your cash flow, reduce bad debts, and raise your profits without alienating your customers.

# HOW TO
# COLLECT
# DEBTS
# (AND STILL KEEP YOUR
# CUSTOMERS)

# Introduction

## Collections—The Big Picture

While Martin was working early one morning on a speech about accounts receivable management for a group of medical administrators, his six-year-old son, Robert, asked him what he was doing. Martin replied that he was preparing a talk to help doctors collect more money. Robert asked, "What do doctors need money for?" Martin said, "They have to pay nurses, buy medical equipment, pay rent, and a lot of other things." He added that it takes a lot of money to keep a doctor's office going.

Robert thought for a moment and then suggested that the doctors do what his Mommy does when she needs money. When Martin asked him to continue he said, "When Mom needs money, she puts Emily, Amanda, and me in the car and we drive to a bank. There are these machines next to the bank. Mom puts in her card, pushes a button, and all this money comes out."

Well, we all know that increasing cash flow is not that simple. There is no single button to push. Every year thousands of businesses file for protection under the bankruptcy laws. Businesses just like yours. It just doesn't seem fair. You have a great product or service. You have a detailed business plan. Sales are exceeding expectations. There's only one problem: You are running out of cash. You cannot pay your bills with profit. You must have cash to pay your bills, and you can't do that if your cash is tied up in your accounts receivable. And to make matters worse, some of your biggest and best customers are your slowest payers. How do you collect your money on time and not run off your best customers? How do you get people to pay as they promised?

Collections are critical to your survival! Reading this book can save your business or, at the very least, it can show you how to make your business more liquid and produce more profits. The main objective of *How to Collect Debts (and Still Keep Your Customers)* is to show you how to collect the most money, as fast as you can, net of expenses, while maintaining the goodwill of the debtor. Let's examine the various components of this objective:

• The most money: This component is self-explanatory.

• As fast as you can: Naturally, you want to get money into your cash flow as quickly as possible.

• Net of expenses: It makes no business sense to spend more money to collect a debt than the debt is worth. It's foolish to adopt the attitude, "I don't care what it costs—I just want my money." If the objective of a business is to make a profit, then to lose money collecting a debt is illogical. Your goal should be to collect money, not to teach your debtor a lesson.

• While maintaining the goodwill of the debtor: You'll be much better off if you collect your debt without antagonizing your debtor or making him hostile. It doesn't do you or your business any good to have a debtor walking around who hates you. All of us in business work hard to build good reputations, and an angry customer, no matter how unjustifiable his anger, can hurt you. He may try to get even by bad-mouthing you or by countersuing. It's unrealistic to think you can collect all of your debts without ever making anyone angry, but it's worth your while to avoid a war and collect your debts amicably.

The major difference between this book and any other on collections is that in this book we concentrate on the big picture. We teach you not only how to collect your bad debts from slow or nonpayers, but how to avoid them. Bad debts are generally a symptom of another problem. We personally own and operate businesses that have required us to become masters of credit and collections to survive. We have learned to look at collections from a total business standpoint. When you have delinquencies, it's necessary for you to examine your entire business, not just blame your collection department.

While most people think that the collection process begins when an account first becomes past due, nothing could be further from the truth. Collections begin the moment you make contact with your customers—through your ads, when you first talk to them on the phone, or when you meet them in person. You must take a good credit application, verify the information on the application, clearly explain your expectations of payment, make sure the first payment is made on time, and provide an exceptional product or service so that customers will want to pay as promised. If your delinquencies are higher than they should be, it's because you and your employees are doing something to cause these delinquencies.

## Always Ask for Your Money!

Many business people and professionals are simply afraid to ask for their money. They fear that their customer, client, or patient will be offended and run to the competition. But think about it. Your customer knows when she chooses your product or service that she is expected to pay. It is you and your employees who are usually responsible for creating slow or no payers, or bad debt. At our seminars, we always pose the question: Who likes to ask for money? Very few people raise their hands because most people don't like to ask. But you're not going to get what you don't ask for. Everyone feels like he is the last to be paid, but the last person to be paid is the last person to ask.

It should be obvious, then, that *ask* is the most important word in collections. You must persistently and consistently ask for your money. And you should start asking the second you make contact with your potential customer. We don't mean that you should walk up to a prospect you've just met and say, "Give me all of your money." We do mean that you should start setting the stage from the very beginning. We've written this book to help you do that, and more.

To those ends, we have divided the book into three sections:

1. **A**ttitude
2. **S**peed
3. **K**nowledge

The first letters of these section titles conveniently spell ASK. If you always ask for your money, you will collect more money and you will increase your sales volume, too.

## Attitude

If you don't maintain a collection attitude in your business or practice, your cash flow suffers. The consequences often are catastrophic. If I were a banker and a customer came to me asking to increase his line of credit, I'd first have him examine his accounts receivable to see whether more cash could be generated. But the average business owner will tell you that his accounts receivable is fine and that his customers pay their bills—they just pay "a little slow." However, "a little slow" can put you out of business.

In this section we give you an overall feel or attitude about collections. We're talking about your attitude, not the debtor's. You need to understand why your business has collection problems, how important credit is to our economy and society, and that the whole credit system would not work without bill collectors. You need to know how important it is to have an assumptive attitude when you collect a debt, to believe in where you work, and to run an exceptional business. You must also realize it's important to treat your accounts receivable as if it were your own and to try to negotiate a win–win solution with your debtor.

### Speed

In the second section, we explain that time is the weapon of the debtor—the longer it takes you to collect, the less likely it is you will be successful.

### Knowledge

In the final section, we discuss how knowledge of credit policies and appropriate customer contact through collection letters, telephone calls, and personal visits affect collection results. We demonstrate how to collect accounts when you have limited resources, provide information about collection attorneys and collection agencies, and show you how to evaluate outside collection services. Finally, we tell you how you can make collections more palatable by using competition and keeping score.

## A Note to the Reader

It's important that you understand the difference between commercial and consumer collections. A commercial collection is the collection of a debt from another business. A consumer collection is the collection of a debt from an individual. Medical fees collected from a patient would be considered a consumer collection. In this book we use the word *consumer* to mean customer, patient, or client.

Some people feel that commercial collections (business to business collections) and consumer collections are totally different. This idea is not true. Most of the same principles, practices, and policies that work for one type of collection will work for the other.

# Section One

# **Attitude**
# S
# K

In this section we cover the following topics:

- Why you have bad debts
- What if there were no credit and no bill collectors?
- Why you must have an assumptive attitude
- Why you must believe in where you work
- How important it is to run an exceptional business
- Why you must treat money you're collecting as if it were your own
- Why you should negotiate a win—win collection

Understanding the relationships between these topics and collections will help you develop an appropriate attitude about asking for money that is due you.

# Why You Have Bad Debts

*Never tell a debtor that his bill is outstanding,*
*he may think it's a compliment.*
*—Anonymous*

Your collection or credit department doesn't operate in a vacuum, and your bad debts are not an isolated part of your business. If you blame your credit and collection department for all of your past due accounts, you aren't looking at the entire picture. Everyone in your organization must understand how their roles affect the collection of accounts receivable and act accordingly.

## Who Do You Blame?

In spite of modern medical advances, there are a lot of seriously ill people in America today. Whose fault is it? Do we blame the doctors? No, doctors don't cause people to be sick. It's their responsibility to treat patients and make them well. The question we should be asking is, Why are all these people unhealthy in the first place? Maybe it's because they smoke or drink too much. Maybe it's because they take drugs. Maybe they don't eat the right foods. So if an individual wants to avoid bad health, he might consider changing his lifestyle—not blaming his doctor.

What do doctors and sick patients have to do with your bad debts? Let's assume that your bad debts last year were $60,000. This year they're up to $100,000, and you still have a few more delinquent accounts that could raise this figure even higher. Should you condemn your collection department?

Just as it is the responsibility of doctors to treat sick patients, it's the responsibility of your collection staff to treat ailing accounts. But why do you have so many unhealthy accounts? Maybe your salespeople are not properly explaining the payment terms to your customers. Maybe *your* desire for increased sales forces your credit department to extend credit to unworthy debtors. Maybe your product or service is inferior and your customers are not motivated to pay.

None of these problems are the fault of your collection department. If your company has a well-thought-out credit and collection plan with the appropriate policies and procedures in place, and if everyone in your organization plays their role properly, you will have fewer accounts in intensive care for your collection department to deal with.

Maybe your company needs a lifestyle change.

## Let's Blame Anne

Anne attended one of our seminars on collections. She arrived thirty minutes early and sat in the front row. She was the collection manager of a small but growing company whose bad debts were out of control, and the owner was applying a lot of pressure to eliminate delinquencies and reduce days outstanding.

Anne never moved from her chair. She took notes. She asked questions. She absorbed everything. Never in all the years that we've been putting on seminars have we had a participant who seemed more motivated to learn. So we were totally surprised at the end of the session when she came up and said that we hadn't been much help. Consequently, we asked her to stay afterward so we could review her specific problem.

## Company Survey

We surveyed the following areas of her business to determine where she had gone wrong:

- Personnel
- Credit criteria and approval
- Billing practices
- Management reports
- Control of payment arrangements
- Payment incentives and penalties
- Quality of product or service and of complaint handling

### Personnel

As a first step, we reviewed the personnel situation to decide whether a change would be in order. We determined that Anne was not the problem. She was assertive, conscientious, organized, and enthusiastic and was bound and determined to collect *her* money.

## Credit Criteria and Approval

So we moved on to the next area and hit the jackpot. We asked Anne to describe the credit policies of her company. She said that the owner was aggressively trying to grow the business and the company was expanding rapidly. In his desire for growth, the owner, unfortunately, had gotten directly involved in the credit approval process and had relaxed the usual strict criteria. And to make matters worse, when she tried to control the customer's purchases, he often overruled her and approved the credit over her objection.

We suggested that she try to keep the owner out of the credit decision. Owners are generally optimists. They are customer oriented and are anxious to increase sales. Also, if the owner is available to talk to the customer, the customer realizes the owner has the authority to approve the purchase. It is then difficult for him to turn anyone down.

We told her that the company needed to have a *written credit policy*. This policy should spell out who is responsible for writing up the credit application and how it is to be verified, as well as determine who calls the credit references, the bank, and the credit-reporting agency. The policy should state who is responsible for explaining the credit terms to the customer in advance of delivery, how the credit limit is set, and who can approve credit.

Anne told us that the salespeople were responsible for getting the application completed, but she knew they were more interested in making sales and earning commissions than in writing a quality credit application. They were also responsible for explaining the payment arrangements to the customer. She felt that they were afraid to discuss the terms in detail for fear of losing the sale and that the owner would not be willing to make any changes.

## Billing Practices

What happens when a customer misses a payment? How long does she wait to follow up? Does she send mail or call? What does she do when she has determined that she will be unable to collect the balance? She told us she waits until the account is thirty days past due before she sends mail, and then she sends a statement every thirty days thereafter. At ninety days the owner is supposed to review each delinquent account, but is usually so far behind that he doesn't follow through on a timely basis.

We suggested she speed up the collection process and include some telephone calls with the letters. We also recommended that if the owner was not going to be available, she request authority to charge off the account or turn it over to an outside service for collection. However, as we expected, she told us the owner was not open to change.

## Management Reports

Sometimes you don't realize you have a delinquency problem because of inadequate management reports. But if your delinquencies are bad, the job of preparing reports is so overwhelming it seems like an impossible task. We asked Anne about her management reports or other collection tools. She said that she got a printout of all accounts that were thirty, sixty, and ninety or more days past due. She complained that the list was monstrous and included many customers who would ultimately pay, but slower than scheduled.

Because she had to deal with so many accounts, we suggested the company develop some month-end exception reports. The computer could select:

- All the customers whose accounts had undergone a statistically significant unfavorable change.

- Those customers who were chronically behind and needed constant attention.
- The *new* customers who had already missed their first payment. Then she could train the new customers to pay on time before developing bad habits.

We suggested the reports be printed with the larger balances first so the bigger balances would always be covered. An exception report would also allow her to concentrate on the appropriate accounts and not have to waste time trying to review every single past due account.

Anne told us that she had asked the owner for some new reports, and had been told that their computer operated with off-the-shelf software and no changes could be made. He certainly wasn't going to spend money to have the programs rewritten.

### Control of Payment Arrangements

We asked Anne who was responsible for giving customers permission to reduce their payments. She said she had control of this job and was doing fine.

We were glad that she was monitoring the extension of terms closely because giving customers permission to reduce their payments is just another way of cutting prices. It also reduces cash flow and makes you more likely to accumulate bad debts.

### Payment Incentives and Penalties

We asked whether the company had built in any payment incentives or penalties such as cash discounts, discounts for prompt payment, interest, or late charges. She said it was not a common practice in their industry to charge interest or late charges and had been told the company's margins were not large enough to absorb any type of reduction in prices.

### Quality of Product or Service and of Complaint Handling

We asked her about the quality of her company's product and whether her company handled complaints promptly. She said that this area was not a problem. The reason we mentioned this was to eliminate the excuse of a disputed account as a stalling tactic by the customer. These disputed accounts can really slow down collection.

## Conclusion

Anne could sit at our seminar for five days, read ten books on collections, and listen to twenty-five tapes on accounts receivable management and her recoveries would not improve significantly. As the collection manager, she had very little control over those things that could make a difference. She needed to spend some time with the owner and convince him to make some changes.

**Collection departments alone don't cause bad debts— bad management causes bad debts.**

You can't blame the doctor for the number of sick and ailing patients. You also can't necessarily blame your collection department for the large number of sick and ailing accounts. Use the company survey to review your own situation. Make the appropriate changes and maybe your collection department won't have so many accounts to worry about.

# What if There Were No Credit or No Bill Collectors?

*About six months ago my wife lost her credit card. I decided not to report it because the bills came in cheaper.*
*—Anonymous*

## What if There Were No Credit?

You're watching television while your five year-old daughter plays outside. You hear the screech of brakes and a scream, and to your horror, you see your daughter has been hit by a car.

You dial 911 and an ambulance is dispatched. The driver jumps out of his ambulance, but instead of rushing to your daughter, he comes over to you to demand a $250 payment in advance. You beg him to please help your daughter and to send you a bill. He explains that the U.S. Congress has recently passed a bill abolishing credit. All financial transactions from this time forward must be paid

17

in cash. You panic, but then realize that you have the money in your cookie jar.

You throw the cash at the driver and jump into the ambulance with your daughter. You arrive at the hospital, but your daughter is in great pain and crying. You assure her that the doctor will make her feel better and that everything will be all right.

You arrive at the emergency room and rush your daughter inside. You tell the admitting nurse about your daughter's accident and she informs you that she must have $500 cash in advance to cover the deductible and the co-pay. She reminds you that credit is against the law. You have no more cash left—so what do you do?

This is what the world would be like without credit. Most of us take the availability of credit for granted. We expect it. We consider it a right. But if there were no credit, our lives would be much more difficult. Many of us would not be able to afford housing. There would be a lot fewer cars on the road. And we would have to get by with fewer major appliances. Consider what it would be like if you came home from work one day and found that your refrigerator was broken and your food was going bad. If you didn't have any available cash, you would have to throw all your food away and not be able to replace your refrigerator.

How would you start a new business if you had to pay cash for everything? How could any company operate in an all-cash society?

The availability of credit allows us to have a better life and a higher standard of living.

## What if There Were No Bill Collectors?

*I don't get no respect. When I was born I was so ugly,*
*the doctor slapped my mother.*
*—Rodney Dangerfield*

Just like Rodney Dangerfield, bill collectors get no respect. Debtors ignore their letters and avoid their phone calls. People lie to them and threaten them. Even in their own companies, salesmen consider bill collectors killjoys and all the other employees think they should lighten up.

So let's get rid of them. Instead of assuming that Congress mandates an end to credit, let's assume it leaves credit intact, but banishes all bill collectors. Is life great or what? Things don't get any better than this! You can now charge all your purchases as before, but you don't have to worry that some troublesome bill collector will bother you for payment.

This may sound great at first, but what do you think would happen? Do you really think that most people would pay if they knew that no one would call or write? And if many people don't pay, do you think businesses would continue to extend credit as they do now?

We think there would be two major consequences if bill collectors were eliminated: The cost of all goods and services would skyrocket and the availability of credit would collapse.

1. *Businesses would raise prices.* Because bad debts would increase dramatically, every company that offered credit would have to raise its prices to cover its losses. There is no such thing as a free lunch. When those who consume goods and services fail to pay as they promise, those who do honor their promises pay more.

It is estimated by the American Collectors Association that bad debts written off each year by U.S. businesses amount to $375 for every man, woman, and child in America. That's $1,500 extra a family of four must pay for goods and services every year. In addition, more than one and a half million checks are bounced daily. Can you imag-

ine how much more honest people would have to pay if
there were no bill collectors?

2. *Credit would be difficult to get.* Businesses would extend a lot less credit. Credit would be difficult to get because the credit approval process would be intensified.
Every applicant would be scrutinized closely. The creditor
would demand a stronger credit application and the application would be held to the highest standards. Consequently, businesses would extend a lot less credit.

## Conclusion

Being able to buy on credit improves our lives. It raises
our standard of living. It allows us to buy things that we
would otherwise not be able to afford. But we also must
appreciate the vital role bill collectors play. Without bill
collectors, our credit system would be crippled.

So the next time you have to collect a bill, just remember how important you are to our credit system. Nothing
would work without you.

# The Assumptive Attitude

*The kindergarten teacher was inspecting the drawings of her students. She went over to a little girl who had just picked up her crayons and was beginning her task. The teacher asked the young child what she was going to draw. The little girl responded that she was going to paint a picture of God. "A picture of God?" replied the teacher, "No one knows what God looks like." The little girl answered, "Not until now."*
*(Example of a positive assumptive attitude)*

## Personal Expectations

People often get what they expect. A dramatic negative example of this observation is the story of Elvis Presley's premature death. Elvis died when he was forty-three years old, at the same age, of the same condition, and in almost the same month that his mother died many years before. During his last few months of life, Elvis was obsessed that he might die at the age of forty-three just like his mother.

As a contrasting example, let us tell you about an employee we hired for a collection position a number of years ago. The story is even more revealing when you realize that this new employee had never had any collection experience. After she had completed about a week of training, the collection manager told her to pick up a stack of delinquent accounts and start calling. (This was in the year B.C.—"before computers"—when all accounts were collected on ledger cards.)

You have never seen such energy and enthusiasm. The collector-in-training was like a child with a new toy. She was motivated and determined to prove herself. She grabbed the phone and talked as she had never talked before. She begged. She pleaded. She methodically contacted each debtor and sold them on the benefits of payment. She found new addresses. She found new phone numbers. And she collected a lot of money.

The remarkable thing is that this novice collector had inadvertently picked up the wrong stack of accounts. She had called a group of debtors who had been placed on the collection manager's desk to be charged off and filed away. These accounts had already been worked by the collection pros, and it had been determined that these accounts were totally "uncollectable."

The only reason that this new employee had succeeded was she didn't know the accounts couldn't be collected. If someone had said, "Go over there and grab that stack of accounts. They have already been thoroughly worked. They are impossible to collect and you will probably be wasting your time." How successful do you think she would have been?

## I Know I Can . . . I Know I Can

*A man jumps off the top of the World Trade Center and around the 50th floor says, "Well, so far, so good."*
*(An example of a positive assumptive attitude)*

During our collection seminars we usually ask the following riddle:

> **RIDDLE: What's the difference between a .250 hitter and a .300 hitter in baseball?**
> **ANSWER: About $10 million.**

The .250 hitter thinks he can get a hit once every four times at bat. The .300 hitter plans to get a hit every time. Naturally the baseball superstar doesn't bat 1.000, but he performs at a high level because of his assumptive attitude.

This thinking is also the difference between a superstar collector and an average one. Over the past twenty years, we have hired many collectors and there is one trait that is common to all the best: They all assume they are going to be successful.

Have you ever met a person who is so self-assured that he thinks he can accomplish anything? That usually describes the successful collector. You tell him that he can't do something and he tries to prove to you that he can. You know the children's story about the train that says, "I think I can . . . I think I can"? The really great collector with an assumptive attitude says, "I know I can . . . I know I can."

## Conclusion

A collector must have a positive attitude. When was the last time you saw anyone accomplish anything when he was sure that he would fail? The average baseball player will hit .250 because he doesn't think he's going to get a hit every time. The megabucks baseball player is going to be a star because he expects to get a hit every time. Babe Ruth pointed to the fence and hit a home run.

In 1969, Joe Namath shook up the sports world when

he predicted that his upstart New York Jets of the fledgling American Football League would win the Super Bowl. Even though the Jets were 17- to 19-point underdogs, Joe Namath stepped up to the podium and said, "I'm going to tell you, we're going to win. I guarantee it." And his team did the impossible: they won 16–7.

Top-notch collectors *know* they will be successful. This is the assumptive attitude.

# Believe in Where You Work

*A woman went to the bank to cash her husband's paychech. "It needs an endorsement," the teller explained. The woman thought for a moment, then wrote on the back of the check, "Sam is a wonderful husbund."*

## You, Too, Can Love Garbage

Tom Peters, the author of the book *In Search of Excellence* also produced a video by the same name. In this video Peters tells about a man named Len Steffanelli and his company, Sunset Scavengers. Sunset Scavengers is the San Francisco Garbage Company. According to the video, it is one of the best managed companies in America.

"You ask Lenny what his secret is and he says it's simple. He says, 'I love garbage.' And he does. He loves his garbage as much as Dr. Wang [the forerunner to Bill Gates] loves his computers. His office is a joy. His office is [filled with] ceramic pigs and porcelain garbage cans and porcelain garbage trucks and he loves it!"

There is no doubt that Mr. Steffanelli believes in what he does and in where he works. If he can love garbage, then it shouldn't be that difficult for you to love what you do.

In Chapter 3 we expressed the importance of believing in yourself. It's equally important that you believe in where you work. Your company provides a worthwhile product or service. If it didn't, your business wouldn't survive. Every time your customers or clients choose to do business with you, they verify the importance of your existence.

I would like to illustrate my point by describing two of the businesses we own and operate.

## Unglamorous Business 1

### AmSher Collection Services

James Collins and Jerry Porras, in their book, *Built to Last,* recommend that all great companies have a BHAG—A Big Hairy Audacious Goal. Our BHAG at AmSher is:

**To become the best accounts receivable management company in the world.**

We will accomplish our goal by honoring our core values. We will have a strong mission, a vision, and a purpose, and we will concentrate on our strengths.

Our *core values* are:

- *Honesty*—Always tell the truth.
- *Dignity*—Treat all people with dignity and respect.
- *Continuous improvement*—We will always find ways to improve.

Our *mission* is to enhance the value of our clients' companies by providing innovative services that convert their receivables into cash, so they can focus their energies and resources on core competencies.

Our *vision* is to be a company that listens, understands, and responds with a sense of urgency. We will treat everyone with honesty, respect, and a smile. We will continue to improve. We will accept nothing less.

Our *purpose* is to solve our clients' problems.

Our *strengths* are:

- accounts receivable management technology
- telephone collections
- recruiting, training, and motivating exceptional people
- living our core values

Every year we collect millions of dollars for our clients. If we didn't recover this money, our clients would have to raise prices to make up for those people who didn't pay; extend less credit; earn less money and be less competitive; and lose money and possibly go out of business.

We recently sent five collectors (our collection SWAT team) to a major bank for ninety days to make collection calls for one of their divisions. According to their executive vice-president, we cut their delinquencies from 8 percent to 4 percent, and saved the bank between $3 and $4 million in bad debts. We also are making customer service calls for a local utility before termination of service for lack of payment and have cut their number of disconnects by 50 percent.

The employees at AmSher take a great deal of pride and satisfaction in saving customers and in recovering money that would have otherwise been lost. Are we at AmSher proud of what we do? You bet we are!

## Unglamorous Business 2

### Mr. King Furniture

We at Mr. King Furniture willingly extend credit to people whom our competition have rejected because the probability of payment is low. Do we at Mr. King serve a useful purpose? You bet we do! What is our value? We give people with no credit or bad credit an opportunity to establish or reestablish their credit. We raise the standard of living for thousands of low- and moderate-income people by giving them the opportunity to own name-brand furniture, appliances, and televisions.

You might say that an individual with bad credit doesn't deserve a second chance. Maybe you're right, maybe you're not. Oftentimes life plays dirty tricks on honest people with good intentions. Our potential customer may have been injured in an automobile accident or become seriously ill and been unable to pay her medical bills. She might have unexpectedly been laid off her job during a downturn in the economy. Her car may have required sudden and costly repairs or her house might need a new roof.

What happens when this person tries to cook dinner and finds that the stove is inoperable? If no business is willing to extend credit to her, should her family be relegated to eating cold meals and sandwiches until enough money can be saved to buy a new one?

The employees at Mr. King feel good about helping people get what they want. They feel it is their responsibility to teach customers about credit, budgeting, and planning to improve the customer's options in the future. We, therefore, have many repeat customers who choose to remain loyal to us because we took a chance on them when no one else would give them the time of day.

Our employees are proud of Mr. King Furniture and enjoy helping people. Therefore, they don't mind asking for their money.

## Conclusion

Now let's look at your business. What products or services do you provide? Maybe you work for a doctor who saves people's lives. Maybe you work for a cable company that for a few cents a day provides a wide variety of television entertainment. Maybe you work for a bank that lends money to entrepreneurs who are driven to fulfill their life-long dream of building a business. You might finance cars or houses, but the result is the same. Your business is valuable and worthwhile. You are helping people. And because you make your product or service available on credit, you make it more affordable.

It has been said, "Find a job that you like and believe in and you will never have to work another day in your life." If you *believe in where you work,* you'll feel good about what you do. You'll be enthusiastic and happy. And you'll collect more money.

# Run an Exceptional Business

*Even though I owe a fortune, I have a lot to be thankful
for. At least I'm not one of my creditors.*
*—Anonymous*

## Hoop Jumpers

Several years ago I attended a comprehensive program
for owners of small companies at the Graduate School
of Business at Harvard University. Our marketing profes-
sor warned that many of us had become "hoop jumpers."
Hoop jumpers, he explained, are companies that offer a
product or service similar to those being offered by their
competitors. Hoop jumpers are selling a commodity.

Therefore, every time a customer makes a demand,
we have to jump through their hoop. If they ask us to drop
our prices 5 percent, we get nervous and cut our prices. If
they ask us to prepay the freight, we immediately write a
check to the trucking company. If they tell us that they are
giving themselves an extra thirty days to pay, then we say,
"Take as long as you want." The threat is always the same:

"If you don't do what I demand, then I will take my business to one of your competitors."

Naturally you want to do everything in your power to please your customers. But you don't want to be in a position that every time one of your customers says, "Jump," your response has to be, "How high?"

How do you avoid becoming a hoop jumper? What separates you from your competition so that you maintain some kind of balance of power with your customers? Your solution is to run an exceptional business. You want to operate your business in such a way that your customer or client perceives that your competitor's product or service cannot be substituted for yours.

## "No Cones" Is a Bad Sign

Here's a story about a business that is less than exceptional. One time David and his wife, Ina-Mae, went out for Chinese food. After they finished their meal, they spotted a well-known ice cream shop and decided to go in for dessert. There was a big sign on the window that said SPECIAL—BANANA ROYALE $1.49.

Once inside they got in line behind a young mother and her two children. A teenage boy behind the counter was taking the woman's order. She asked for three ice cream cones and was told that the store was all out of cones. (Can you imagine a national ice cream chain with no cones?) The lady shrugged her shoulders and settled for three ice creams in a cup. This was not a good sign, but David and Ina-Mae fearlessly walked up to the counter anyway.

Ina-Mae asked the young man to tell her about the special. He described the Banana Royale as two scoops of ice cream, bananas, hot fudge, whipped cream, and a cherry. Ina-Mae doesn't like bananas, but she loves hot fudge sundaes. She figured that since the Banana Royale was less expensive than a hot fudge sundae, she would order a Banana Royale and tell the teenager to leave out the bananas.

To her surprise, the young man told her he couldn't do that. He said that if he left off the bananas, he would be serving a hot fudge sundae and he would have to charge her full price for the sundae.

Ina-Mae is not easily deterred, so after a moment of silence, she requested that he put the bananas in a separate cup. He refused. So she asked him to put the bananas under the ice cream. He refused again. By this time, Ina-Mae's patience had worn thin and she asked that he give her one good reason why he couldn't serve the bananas on the side. He replied that he was out of bananas.

Well, David couldn't stand by idly any longer. He stepped in front of his wife and demanded to see the manager. The young fellow informed him that he couldn't. In disbelief David asked him why. He said that the manager was at the grocery store buying bananas.

Now this story sounds unbelievable, but it is true. It is the perfect example of how not to run an exceptional business.

## Above and Beyond

Really great companies set standards well above those of their competitors. I talked previously about Tom Peters' book and video, *In Search of Excellence*. His follow-up book, *A Passion for Excellence*, tells about the time Ray Kroc of McDonald's visited a Winnepeg franchise. "It's reported that he found a single fly. The franchisee lost his McDonald's franchise two weeks later."

Another great company is Southwest Airlines. Southwest continues to grow and make money year after year while the growth of most other airlines is cyclical. Southwest is consistently rated first for on-time performance, fewest complaints, and the least amount of luggage lost. It is repeatedly selected as one of the top companies in America to work for, and its employees are enthusiastic and happy. The flight attendants sing to you and tell jokes. For example, on a flight David recently took to New Orleans, the flight attendant came on the public address system as the plane was taxiing up to the terminal. She said she had a special announcement to make. "A man is celebrating his 100th birthday on board today and who has never flown before." Everyone on the plane clapped and cheered. She then told us to "congratulate the pilot on the way out."

Then there's the retail legend Parisian (now a division of Saks), which was founded in Birmingham. Parisian is a department store that in 1963 had only one location in the central business district. Today it is expanding rapidly and is opening stores all over the country. What is so special about Parisian?

Parisian has a commitment to service that is reflected in two unique competitive advantages: It offers the option of six months' free credit and has the unique reputation of allowing customers to return merchandise with no questions asked.

This "easy return" policy has personally cost David a fortune. His wife, Ina-Mae, often goes to the ladies' department and picks out three or four dresses. Unable to decide which one to buy, she takes them all. Why not? She knows she can return them whenever she pleases. Unfortunately for David, he suspects that many times she keeps them all. There is no telling how much extra merchandise Parisian sells this way.

Emil Hess, one of the founders of Parisian, told a story that exemplifies his company's commitment to this winning policy. A young lady came into Parisian to return a pair of designer jeans. The clerk realized that the jeans were not purchased there and told the manager. The manager, who was new on the job, explained to the young woman that since the jeans had been bought elsewhere, he could not take them back.

The girl went home and complained to her father who angrily wrote a letter to Mr. Hess accusing Parisian of mistreating his daughter. When Mr. Hess received the letter, he went to the store to discuss the matter with the manager. After reviewing the details, the manager decided that he would not only take back the jeans and return the money, but he would drive to the girl's house personally to satisfy the complaint.

When we tell retail store owners this story, many of them get upset and tell us this is bad business. "You can't allow customers to return merchandise they didn't buy from you." But Parisian has been wildly successful following this unorthodox policy.

Mr. Hess believed that most people are honest. When you doubt their honesty by refusing to take back their merchandise, you make them angry. If the personnel at Parisian have to sort out the reasonable returns from the unreasonable returns, they take the chance of upsetting many customers. Why not make it easier on the employees and the customers by not doubting anyone? This unique policy has separated Parisian from its competitors and has allowed Parisian to prosper while many other department stores have failed.

## Conclusion

What does all this have to do with collections? You want your customers to think they have to do business with you.

David's wife does most of her shopping at Parisian even though there are probably ten other stores in our city with comparable merchandise. If your customers believe that they can buy the identical product from many different sources, they operate from a position of power and may try to dictate the terms and conditions of sale. You reduce your customers' power when you are the only perceived choice.

Participants at our seminars are always telling us they are afraid to ask their customers to pay on time for fear of losing them to the competition. We feel this is an irrational fear, and psychologically it may put you at a disadvantage. If you offer your customers something unique, however, they can't be so independent. If your customers feel your company is the only company they want to do business with, then they have to play and pay according to your rules.

Run an exceptional business. Your sales will increase and you will collect more money.

# Treat Money to Be Collected as if It Were Your Own

## Build Urgency!

In the workplace we usually find employees who are trying to collect money for someone else—their employers. To understand the difference that a sense of urgency can make in collections, here's an account by Martin of a technique we use in our "Championship Collections" seminars:

At every seminar I pull a brand new $5 bill out of my wallet, wave it above my head, and promise to give it to the first person who brings me $20. Usually two or three people grab their wallets or purses and race to the front of the room with their money.

I thank the winner and take his $20 and my $5 and promptly put the money in my wallet. Then I ask the lucky winner to please sit back down so I can continue. He usually hesitates, grumbles about something or another, and then slowly returns to his seat. I reassure him that I will return his money plus the $5 reward, but he needs to be patient. (I always hope that the lucky winner is a lot smaller than I am.)

I hold onto the cash for a few minutes, but those few minutes demonstrate an important point. When you are trying to collect your own money, your attitude, your aggressiveness, the urgency of the situation is totally different than when you are trying to collect someone else's money. You want your money back now!

After I return the money to the winner, I again ask for volunteers. (Of course no one trusts me this time.) Then I ask for people to raise their hands if they are employees of a business—not the owners. I ask them to please leave their hands raised if their paycheck is important to them. I mean *really* important! I only want a volunteer who has to pay the rent, buy groceries, and pay bills, and who will be in serious trouble if his check doesn't come on payday. I usually find that includes almost everyone in the room.

I then choose one person to role-play with me. I tell the individual that I will be the boss and she will be one of my employees. We are going to assume that it's payday. I phone the employee at work from my home and explain to her that my children are sick, that my wife is out of town, and that I won't be able to come into work today to sign her payroll check. Is that okay?

This is obviously not acceptable, so I ask her to brainstorm ways to get her check signed and into her hands immediately. Her suggestions might include:

"I'll babysit—you come in and sign the check."

"I could get my mother to come sit for you."

"Send the kids to school . . . they'll feel better later."

"I know a doctor who makes house calls."

"I'll have a courier service deliver the check to you."

This employee must have her money this morning. She can't wait until next week. She can't wait until tomorrow. She can't even wait until tonight. She has to have it now. Yet this same employee may pick up the phone a few minutes later and ask a customer, "When do you want to pay on your account?" One week, two weeks, even a month later is okay. What's the difference? The difference is that when it's your paycheck, you have to have it right away—it's urgent. When it's someone else's paycheck, you can afford to be much more generous.

That's why business owners and their spouses can often be so effective at collecting money. It's not that they are better collectors, it's just that they are a lot more motivated. It's their own money.

## Conclusion

If you are going to be an effective collector, you have to go after the money as if it were your own. If you have the attitude that it's yours, you will be quicker to ask for the money. You will be much more assertive. You'll be much more creative. And, consequently, you will be more successful.

# Win–Win Negotiations

*Before it was purchased by Time Warner, Paragon*
*Cable of New York City reported that collection of*
*overdue bills improved dramatically when the company*
*stopped punishing customers who owed money by cutting*
*off service. Instead, deadbeat subscribers had their*
*signals locked on C-SPAN.*
*—Forbes, July 6, 1998*

## Maintaining the Goodwill of the Debtor

Here's the story of two friends who had been in business together as equal partners for many years. When one of them made a decision to retire, he didn't want to jeopardize their friendship by fighting over the business. One partner agreed to set the selling price of the company and the other agreed to set the terms of the sale. Then each drew straws to determine who would be the buyer and who would be the seller.

This is a good example of win–win negotiations. Since neither partner knew which one would end up the owner, each tried to structure as fair a deal as possible. Consequently, a very large business deal was consummated and the two longtime partners remained friends.

If the debt collection effort is handled properly, both parties to that process should also remain friends. Remember, your objective should be to collect the most money as fast as you can, net of expenses, while maintaining the goodwill of the debtor. Keep in mind that most people are honest and intend to pay. On average 80 percent of the people who owe you money will pay on time; 18 percent intend to pay as promised, but are unable to do so for one reason or another; and 2 percent are "credit criminals" who never intended to pay.

Forget the "credit criminals"—you aren't going to collect your money from them anyway. And you certainly don't have to worry about the 80 percent who are going to pay as agreed. So almost all of your collection effort will be directed at the 18 percent who have good intentions, but who are unable to pay on time.

If your debtor has good intentions, you gain nothing by antagonizing him. Experience has probably shown you that when you tell someone that they have to do something, they usually go out of their way to prove to you that they don't have to do anything that they don't want to do.

The fact is that both of you have a problem. Your problem is that you have to have your money now. His problem is that he is unable to pay or doesn't want to pay right now. You resolve your conflict by convincing the debtor that you are on his side and that it is in his own best interest to pay as agreed. The debtor usually makes the decision to pay after he adds up the pluses and minuses and decides that he is better off paying than not paying.

We try to hire good salespeople as collectors because a collector's job is to sell the debtor on the benefits of payment. There is one major difference, however, between collectors and salespeople. The collector must make the sale. To not pay is not an option. So, how do you maintain the goodwill of the debtor and still collect your money? How do you make the debtor feel good about paying?

The following article which appeared in our local newspaper, documents a cooperative approach:

## Banks Using Gentle Videos to Get Debtors to Repay Bills

**By Karen Gullo**
*THE BIRMINGHAM NEWS*

AUGUST 13, 1994, — For people who've fallen behind in their credit card bills, the era of stiff warning and repeated phone calls requesting payment may be coming to an end.

Some big banks have successfully experimented with a gentler approach—mailing deadbeats a kindly, "we feel your pain" videotape that beseeches them to confer with a credit officer and set up a reasonable repayment schedule.

Chase Manhattan Corp. began sending a tape to hundreds of customers this month, featuring a silky-voiced actor who plays a bank representative saying "Hey, it's OK" and "Together, we can work it out." He repeatedly urges delinquents to call an 800 number on the screen.

Banc One has been sending a tape to 1,000 customers a month. AT&T's credit card subsidiary plans a video test of its own. The practice is gaining attention at other banks and credit card companies.

Exuding empathy instead of nastiness to get late-payers back on track is a novelty in the collection business. But it evidently is working for

Chase, the nation's fifth-largest issuer of Visa and MasterCards.

Customers who call the bank will be treated with dignity and not raked over the coals, says the seven-minute video, which cost the bank $27,000 to produce and $3.50 each to mail.

"We're doing more than trying to get money," says a Chase collections agent, one of several real Chase employees giving testimonials to the bank's dedication. "We're trying to help people to get out of a financial problem."

Another agent recounts a conversation with a delinquent customer facing financial trouble because her husband left her.

"He left her with the bills," the agent says. After discussing her problem, the woman felt better. "She said, 'Thank you so much, I'm so glad I talked to you.'"

## The Proof Is in the Appreciation

An effective collector should be able to collect the debt and have the debtor thank him or her. We have had debtors show their appreciation to our collectors by sending them cakes, cookies, candy, thank-you notes, and cards. We do have to admit that some of us on occasion have been reluctant to bite into some of these surprise goodies, but we're happy to announce that to date we have not lost a single collector from our debtors' gifts.

Here are five sample thank-you letters that our collectors have received from debtors (the names, of course, have been changed). These letters show that understanding, empathy, and sincerity are important in win–win negotiations.

*Hi Jo,*

*Thank you so much for being the special person you are. Thanks for helping Mr. Foster and me with our account.*

*We are doing fine now. Keep us in your prayers and thoughts. We really fought a battle for a while, but with God's help and people like you, maybe we will have that battle won. We seek strength daily, for it isn't an easy battle.*

*Enclosed are a few of my favorite poems. Thought you might like and enjoy them.*

*Always,*

*Mr. & Mrs. Edward Foster*

---

*To Mary,*

*Thanks very much.*

*There should be an award for understanding. You are a wonderful person. In our lifetime we've only met a few! Have a very happy day.*

*Mr. & Mrs. John Williams*

*Dear Mrs. Latham,*

*Enclosed please find a check in the amount of $80.00. Mrs. Latham, God bless you for ever and ever! And I mean this from my heart! I thank you so very much for understanding the situation I am going through. I never expected things to go this way. . . .*

*. . . I know my credit is ruined and that troubles me, but I just thank God for you . . .*

*Helen Johnson*

---

*Ms. Good:*

*Thank you for your kindness.*

*Enclosed herewith please find my check in the amount of $2,666 to settle my account.*

*I'm so sorry that it has not been paid already but this year has been like a nightmare for our family. Please believe me because I'm not just making excuses.*

*All of us have a rainbow but we have to paint it with the colors that have been allotted to us. I pray that you have bright beautiful colors to paint your rainbow today.*

*Sincerely,*

*Agnes Washington*

*Ms. Walters:*

> *This is to acknowledge our conversation held this day.*

> *Enclosed is the post-dated check you requested, dated the 31st of July.*

> *Again, I thank you for your kindness and concern exhibited in this matter. I shall continually request that God shower His blessings on you and family, and also, that it may be in a double portion manner. My wife, Linda, and I shall always keep you on our prayer list, and preferably at the top . . .*

> *God bless you and keep you.*

*Respectfully submitted,*

*Rev. & Mrs. Charles Wilson*

These letters are real. It takes a special collector to be able to collect a debt and have the debtor feel good about it. But that should be the objective of every collection effort.

## Conclusion

Earn a PHD in collections. PHD stands for "preserve human dignity." Negotiate with your debtor for a win–win solution. You not only will collect more money, but you will feel better about yourself and your debtor will feel better about you and your company. You earn a PHD in collections by treating your debtors as you want other people to treat you.

# Section Two

# A
# Speed
# K

In this section you will learn the importance of collecting your receivable *quickly*, which is a critical component of running a successful business. By collecting your money *with urgency*, you will collect more money, have less complaints and disputes, and your customers will do more business with you.

# Time Is the Weapon of the Debtor

*Our accounts were so far past due that we aged them by*
*the year rather than by the month.*
—*Anonymous*

## Collectability Time Line

The longer an account remains unpaid, the lower the
probability of collection. According to the International Association of Commercial Collectors and based on
a study by Dun & Bradstreet, among companies that manage receivables internally, the probability of collecting a
payment ninety days past due declines by 12 percent for
each additional thirty-day period. And retaining bad debt
doesn't pay either. A company's probability of collecting is
50 percent greater for a claim that is placed with a collection agency when it is six months past due than when it is
one year past due. Yet, we regularly hear creditors say, "If
I give my debtor enough time, he will probably pay." But
having a debt hanging on is like being a contestant on one
of the first game shows on television. The contestants tried

to stay on the show as long as possible. The longer they remained, the more cash and prizes they won. Their first task, however, was to draw a card out of a box. Listed on this card was an event such as, "the moment that the Greyhound Bus from Syracuse arrives at the bus terminal in Albany," or "the instant that the 53rd person buys a taco at the Mexican restaurant down the street." The very second that the event occurred, the contestants lost all the prizes and money they had accumulated to that point. In the meantime, they were constantly asked, "Do you want to quit now and keep all your prizes, or do you want to continue to play and risk losing everything?"

This is the same risk you face every day when a debtor owes you money. The longer you stay in the game, the greater the risk that some random or not so random event will cause you to lose everything. If you don't recover your money fast enough, you could leave the game empty-handed.

Let's look at the graph shown as Figure 1 that illustrates the value of accounts receivable over time. The vertical axis represents the percentage of debts collected, and the horizontal axis indicates how long it's been since the customer has paid. You'll notice that the potential for collection of the account goes down day by day.

The results of a recent survey of members of the Commercial Collection Agency Section of the Commercial Law League of America show that at three months delinquent, 27 percent of accounts receivable will not be collected. At six months delinquent, 43 percent of accounts receivable will never be recovered, and at twelve months delinquent, nearly 75 percent of delinquent accounts will have to be written off.

Now let's talk specifically about your accounts that are 90 days old or older. There is a tendency for most people to fool themselves into believing that these accounts are

Figure 1   Collectability of delinquent commercial debt. (Copyright Commercial Collection Agency Section, Commercial Law League of America.)

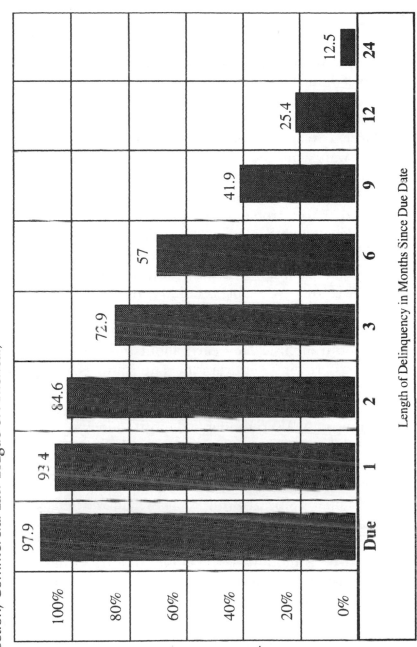

valuable. But what would happen if you went to someone who was totally independent and asked him to set a fair market value?

Let's gather all your ninety-day accounts and take them to your bank. You say to your banker, "Mr. Loan Officer, I've been a good customer of yours for many years and I want you to consider lending me some money, and I want to use this special group of accounts as my collateral." How much money do you think your banker will lend you? You probably won't get a dime.

Many creditors, however, rationalize that if they wait just one more day, they will receive payment. Obviously some debtors will pay, but the odds of payment drop each day. Accounts receivable is not like a fine wine—it does not improve with age.

Several years ago, Martin became interested in investing in a franchise. He heard about this hot new business that was growing very rapidly. The franchiser was getting ready to increase the initial franchise fee by several thousand dollars and one of his salesmen talked Martin into sending a $5,000 refundable deposit to lock in the current fee. While he continued to do research on the company, a friend from California, who coincidentally happened to be a vendor of the franchiser, mentioned that he thought that the company was growing too fast. He warned Martin to be careful.

Martin got nervous and asked the franchise salesman to return his money. He promised that he would return it immediately, but no check arrived. Calls to the accountant, attorney, and owner resulted in excuses and stalls. Martin decided that the only way he would get his money would be to threaten them. He told them that if he didn't get his check by the end of the week he would call their franchisees, their franchise sales organization, and everyone else he could think of and warn them of their company's inability to pay.

He received his money that week and the very next Thursday the franchise bankrupted. If he had waited just one more week, he would have lost his $5,000. Remember that an outstanding receivable is potentially just a day or two away from disaster.

## Lots of Things Can Go Wrong

The longer your debtor owes you money, the more likely that something can go wrong. Just sit back and think of all the things that can happen to your debtor that might prevent him from paying you:

- He could quit his job, get laid off, or be fired.
- He could be called into service by the military reserves.
- He could retire.
- He could get sick, have an accident, or die.
- He could skip or move.
- He could have marital problems—separation or divorce.
- He could file for protection under the bankruptcy laws.
- He could be sued by other creditors who would be ahead of you in a long suit line.

You can suffer similar complications when you try to collect from a business. We have been in business for more than fifty years. We have always been profitable, but we've found that when you go to sleep at night, you never know what you will face the next morning. Here are some catastrophes or near catastrophes that we've had to face:

- a major flood
- fire damage
- termites
- burglaries
- vandalism
- boycott
- a computer conversion that ran amok
- a change in income tax law that significantly acceler-
ated our taxes
- large new competitors came into the market

We are an excellent credit risk. We pay all our bills in
full and on time. But if one of these calamities had caused
us to fail, our creditors would not have been paid. In addition to likewise falling victim to such calamaties, any one of
your business debtors could:

- lose its largest client
- lose its source of financing
- have its assets seized by the Internal Revenue Service
- lose the owner or key employee to sickness or death
- be involved in an earthquake, hurricane, or tornado
- be ruined by a riot
- suffer from employee theft
- be the target of a class action lawsuit

The list is probably endless. In business, as in life,
things can and do go wrong. If we had a nickel for every
one of our collection agency clients who waited until their
debtor had filed Chapter 7 or 11 bankruptcy before turning over an account for collection, we would never have to
work again. Their thinking probably goes something like
this: "Let me try to collect from them one more time and
I'll get the full $1,000 and I won't have to pay the collec-

tion fee." A few days later, the debtor bankrupts and our client ends up with 100 percent of nothing.

## Collect While the Magic Is Still Fresh

It seems to be a rule of human nature that when you do a favor for someone, the value of that service appears to decrease rapidly afterward. The longer people owe you, the more difficult it becomes for them to part with their money. They forget how you helped them by delaying their payment. They look for excuses not to pay and rationalize that something must be wrong with your product or service. Down go your collections and up go your complaints and disputes. David uses a personal experience as an example:

> I'm an avid jogger. One day I was jogging and accidentally stepped off a sidewalk and twisted my ankle. I hit the ground and the pain in my leg was intolerable. I tried to get up, but I couldn't. Fortunately my wife drove by looking for me and spotted me on the side of the road unable to move.
>
> She helped me into the car and we drove to the emergency room of the nearest hospital. A nurse elevated my foot and applied ice to my ankle. After the X rays were developed, I was sent next door to the professional building, where an orthopedic surgeon told me my leg was broken. I was in great pain and I would have paid or done anything to get some relief.
>
> He put my leg into a cast and prescribed some pain medication. Soon I was feeling much better. I was very appreciative. The doctor was

extraordinary. The nurses were angels. Thank
goodness for dedicated medical professionals and
the wonders of medicine.

    A month or two passed and the bills started
rolling in. I got a bill from the emergency room.
I got a bill for the X rays and I got a bill from the
doctor. Wow!!! That sure was a lot of money for a
few minutes of work. The memory of the pain was
beginning to fade. Oh well, it was worth it. I
would file the insurance and not worry about it.

    The accident was a vague memory after a few
months. The insurance company had done its
part, but I was still stuck with the deductible and
co-pay. Now that I think about it, the deductible
and co-pay were more than the doctor and hospital should have charged for everything. So I
thought to myself, "Our medical system is a rip-
off!" These doctors are all out playing golf and
getting rich while us poor working people can
hardly get by. And to make matters worse, my leg
occasionally bothers me. Maybe I should call the
doctor and let him know how unhappy I am.

This story is obviously exaggerated, but it illustrates a
point. At the time of service David was in such pain he
would have paid anything to feel better. But as time went
by, he forgot. Let's just say that the magic had worn off. If
he had been required to pay much earlier in the process,
he may have flinched, but he would have paid and not
worried about it. However, because he still owed the
money, he rationalized reasons for not paying.

    When you are trying to keep your accounts receivable
current, it's important to encourage your customers to pay
while the excitement and enthusiasm of the new product
or service is still fresh. Once it gets stale, so does your customer's willingness to pay.

# Delay Benefits No One

If time is the weapon of the debtor, then why would you give your customers extra time to pay? You might feel that it will be better for your business or better for your customer. Let's examine these perceptions.

## Is It Better for Your Business?

Do you benefit your business in any way by allowing your customers more time to pay?

• False Assumption 1: Your customer will like you better. Let's assume that one of coworkers asks you to loan her $50. She promises to pay you back on payday. You want to help her (after all, isn't that what friends are for?), so you lend her the money. She tells you that she will meet you Friday after work and pay you back. You feel good about yourself for doing such a good deed. You've helped a friend and, who knows, you might need to borrow some money from her one day.

You and your coworker don't run into each other after work and your loan remains unpaid. On Saturday morning you decide to go food shopping at your neighborhood grocery store. Though you are not aware of it, your friend enters the store behind you and spots you pushing your cart down the aisle in the produce section. By the way, she spent most of her paycheck on lottery tickets last night.

Do you think that your friend will:

☐ Rush up to you, hug your neck, and tell you how glad she is to see you?
☐ Duck down another aisle or out the door?

Chances are you and your friend won't run into each other that day.

Have you accomplished your goal of having your supposed friend like you better? And how do you now feel about your friend? You have probably achieved the opposite result. Instead of you and your colleague building and strengthening your relationship, you probably have helped to destroy it.

• False Assumption 2: Your customer will do more business with you. In our retail furniture store we are constantly and persistently trying to collect from our customers. But let's assume that we got a little lax with one of our debtors by allowing him to get a few payments past due. Since we haven't bothered or worried him, do you think that he would like us any better and will shop with us more often?

Let's assume that one of our competitors, Hardnose Furniture Company, doesn't let our common customer get away with a thing. Our strict competitor requires our customer to make every payment in full and on time. Every time this customer misses a payment, Hardnose calls and badgers him into making a payment.

Time marches on and it's now the week before Christmas. Our customer wants to enjoy the holiday season just like the rest of his neighbors. After all, he's worked hard all year. He and his family are entitled to and deserve some presents even though he's seriously past due on his account. So he gathers his family together to go furniture shopping.

Do you think our delinquent customer will:

☐ Shop with us because we have left him alone?
☐ Buy from our competitor, pain-in-the-neck Hardnose Furniture?

He will drive directly to Hardnose. Surprised? You shouldn't be. After all, his credit is good at Hardnose. He's made all his payments. His balance is lower. He is confident that they will be glad to see him.

He really can't buy from us. He's embarrassed that he hasn't paid as promised. His account balance is too high for lack of payment, and he's sure that we don't want to sell to him.

You may be saying to yourself, "Aha! He could outsmart both of you by going to another furniture store." You may be right, but other stores may turn him down because of his slow payment record with us. And to make matters even worse, the debtor will probably be upset and angry with us because he perceives that we ruined his credit.

Hardnose will probably be his only credit option.

Okay—so you agree it's not necessarily better for your business to give your customers extra time to pay, but maybe you are benefiting your customer.

## Is It Better for Your Customer?

• False Assumption 3: You are helping your customers when you allow them to extend their payments. Are you benefiting your customers in any way when you give them extra time to pay? Answer the following two questions:

First, How do you feel when one of your own debts becomes seriously past due?

Do you feel a little apprehensive? Does it hang over your head? Maybe you squirm when the phone rings? Possibly you feel uneasy when you get your mail? Are you worried about what action your creditor might take? Owing a delinquent debt is *stressful*. Being in financial trouble can be an emotionally overwhelming experience.

Second, How do you feel when you pay off a debt? We ask this question at every collection seminar and always get the same response: "I feel relief."

Don't you feel great when you get your car paid off? Wouldn't it feel wonderful to pay off your home? What if you could pay off all your debts?

When you allow a debtor to procrastinate, you make him live with stress and you rob him of that glorious feeling of relief. As the old commercial on television says, "How do you spell relief?" The answer is: Require your customers to p-a-y as a-g-r-e-e-d.

Conversely, your debtor will sustain one more adverse consequence when you let him avoid payment. You allow him to ruin his credit. Many landlords, employers, and financial institutions check credit through their credit bureaus and they will negatively evaluate his credit accordingly.

This is what you have done to your customer by allowing him not to pay:

- Made it impossible for him to be hired.
- Ruined his chances of finding a place to live.
- Made it impossible for him to borrow money.
- Ruined his chances of buying on credit.

- Made him feel nervous, ashamed, or embarrassed.
- Affected him to live under constant stress.
- Made it impossible for him to feel the relief and pleasure of paying off a debt.

This sounds like cruel and unusual punishment.

Do your business and your customers a favor. Require that your customers pay as agreed. You and your customers will be happier.

# A
# S
# Knowledge

In this final section, we share our own knowledge of the following topics:

- How to have fewer bad debts
- How best to utilize collection letters
- When to make a personal visit
- All about collection calls
- What to do when you have limited collection resources
- All about collection agencies and collection attorneys
- How to evaluate and pay outside collection services
- How to make collections fun

Successful collection activities depend on *your* knowledge of credit policies, appropriate customer contact, the use and evaluation of collection services and attorneys, and motivation.

# A Walk Down
# the Avenue

Definition of a *creditor*—A person who has a better
memory than a debtor.

## A Lemonade Story

David is a jogger, and pursuing that activity has pro-
vided him with a number of interesting experiences.
Here's the story of one that seems especially appropriate:

One day last summer, I was jogging in my neighborhood—and it was really hot! I think the tem-
perature was 95 degrees and the humidity was
over 100 percent. Toward the end of the run, I
was getting very, very thirsty. I glanced ahead
and spotted two small boys who appeared to be
about seven or eight years old. They were sitting
in a front yard with a freshly painted sign that
read LEMONADE—25 CENTS. Man, I was so thirsty
I could hardly swallow, but I didn't have any
money. So I shuffled over to the boys and asked,

"Excuse me—do you offer credit?" One boy whispered to his friend, "What's 'credit'?"

I explained that "credit" is when you buy something now, but you pay for it later. So I asked if I could have the drink now, and come back some other time to pay. Even though one of the boys said that would be okay, I wanted to make sure he was comfortable with his decision. So I pointed out the potential problems. I told him that when I came back to pay, he might be gone. What should I do? The boy said to put the money in his mailbox. I told him that I would do that, but no one would be around to watch the mailbox—so someone could come by and take the money.

The bewildered boy looked at his friend and shrugged his shoulders. The other boy hesitated and then turned to him and said, "Oh, why don't we just give it to him?"

Well, I drank my drink, and it was delicious. I walked home and felt guilty. So even though I was tired and could hardly move, I walked back to the lemonade stand. I handed the boy a quarter and a nickel. He looked up at me and asked why I gave him the extra money. I told him that I added some "interest." He replied, "What's 'interest'?"

Many companies have slow pays and bad debts because their customers or clients wear them down. Sometimes, just like these boys, it seems easier to allow your customers to pay at their convenience, or not at all, than to have to deal with them.

## How to Have Fewer Bad Debts

David's story and Chapter 1 provide explanations of why
we have bad debts. Now you'll find out how to avoid them.
Let's take a walk down the A-V-E-N-U-E:

**A**pplication
**V**erification
**E**xpectations
**N**ice courtesy call
**U**rgent first payment
**E**xceptional service

Follow the steps suggested by this acronym. Your delinquencies will fall and your cash collections will increase.

### Application

It's critical that you take a thorough credit application.
Most of you already have some form of credit application,
but you may call it something else. If your application is
used for a medical practice, it might be called a "patient
information form." If it's used by a consulting firm, it
might be called a "client data sheet." Knowledge is power
and the more information you have on your customer or
client the better off you are.

There are three reasons why you want to have a good
credit application:

1. It will help you make a better credit decision.
2. It may come in handy when collecting your account.
3. It could help you increase your sales.

• Better Credit Decision. The information on your application will enhance the quality of your credit decision. You'll have a better idea of whether you want to sell to a customer and you'll set a more suitable credit limit.

Some companies use the information on their application to calculate a credit score. A credit score is created by assigning point values to selected variables to predict a customer's odds of payment. The calculation is usually done by computer. The score allows the credit department to make a decision based on mathematically verifiable facts. This calculation usually provides a better result than an unscientific guess made by an emotional human credit manager. The end result is that you sell less to your worst credit risks and more to your better credit risks.

• Help Collect the Account. The second objective of a good credit application is to provide enough information so that if your customer doesn't pay, you'll still be able to collect.

You might be able to attach a bank account or put a lien on the debtor's property because you have that information listed on the application. Or you might be able to locate a missing debtor because of a previous employment or address that was included.

If you're establishing a line of credit for a business, you might consider adding another section to your credit application to be signed by the company owner to guarantee company payment. This personal guarantee could then be used to prevent the debtor from hiding behind a corporate bankruptcy to avoid payment.

• Increase Your Sales. A well-designed credit application may also help you increase your sales. You can ask marketing questions such as, "How did you hear about our company?" You can then track the responses and adjust your marketing efforts accordingly.

## Verification

Your credit application may be of little or no value if the information on it is inaccurate or incorrect. You'd be surprised at the number of businesses that have their customers fill out applications and then don't bother to see if they've been filled out properly. Often answers are skipped or are illogical. Then, when you need a piece of information to collect the account, the information is not available.

You should definitely verify some of the information on the application. Look in the phone book and see whether you have the correct telephone number or address. Call the business references and find out whether the person or business pays their bills. Gather credit information from credit-reporting agencies, or the credit agency that services your industry. Call the bank reference. Remember that the credit application is of no value if the information on it is wrong or nonexistent.

## Expectations

The couple had just gotten married. It was during the time of the old west and the newlyweds were off to California in their mule-drawn wagon. They traveled a mile or two and their mule suddenly stopped. The bride angrily jumped off the wagon, shook her finger in the face of the mule, and said, "That's one!"

The mule moved forward for a while and then made another sudden stop. Again the woman became furious and shook her finger in the mule's face. She yelled, "That's two!"

They were on their way again, when the mule stopped for the third time. The enraged bride jumped off the wagon and then screamed at the mule, "That's three!" Then she picked up a two-by-four from the side of the road and beat the living stew out of the poor defenseless animal.

She got back in the wagon and the groom said to her, "Honey, I really don't think it was necessary for you to punish old Clyde like that." She turned to him, shook her finger in his face, and said, "That's one!"

The bride in our story really knew how to get her expectations across. Many times, however, businesses do a very poor job of expressing their expectations of payment. As obvious as it may seem, many companies forget to tell their customers when and how much they are supposed to pay. This is a major oversight.

How many times after you've seen the doctor has the bookkeeper informed you that you are to pay at the time of service? Wouldn't it have been nice if someone had told you when you made your appointment? Many companies simply never let the customer in on the secret. How can you get angry with your customer for not paying as agreed when she never agreed to anything?

When Martin's daughter Emily was about six years old and had just learned to play basketball, he and his wife went to one of her games. The coach was required to play all of the children, so he sent a child onto the court who had never played before and had been unable to attend practice. The confused and uncoached child grabbed the ball and started running without dribbling. The coach yelled at her. The parents yelled at her. Even the referee yelled at her. But how was the poor child supposed to know what to do? No one ever told her anything.

This happens every day in business. The customer doesn't pay because no one explained the rules of the game. The customer is then reprimanded by everyone in sight for her ignorance.

To emphasize our point, here are two examples from Martin's personal experiences:

> I have an exercise bicycle that I ride two or three days a week. It needed some repair, so I called the bike shop. We made arrangements so I'd be home when they picked up and returned the bike. As it turned out, I couldn't get off work when they returned the bicycle, so I had my son stay home to let them in. The deliveryman asked for payment at time of delivery and got upset when my son didn't have the money. I had assumed that I would be billed. The bike shop had talked to me on two different occasions, but not once did they say anything about when they expected payment.

> I once signed up for a TV advertising workshop. It was being taught by the owner of a small advertising agency. The course was to meet once a week for six weeks at a local television studio. When I called the instructor, she told me that the cost was $200. She was limiting the class to the first twenty students who registered, and required a $50 deposit. She did a good job of getting across her expectation of payment of the deposit and I immediately sent her a check. She didn't, however, say a word about the remaining $150 balance.

> She didn't mention payment at the first or second class, but on the third week she handed each of us an invoice. She still didn't tell us when she expected payment and she didn't write a due date on the invoice. She left it to our imagination

and good judgment. I assumed that she wanted her money before the last class and I mailed her a check two days before our final meeting.

I got a frantic call from her the morning of the last day of class. She said she had to have payment at class tonight because she had to pay the television studio.

I told her that I had mailed the check a couple of days before and that she would probably get it in the mail today. She said in a joking manner, "It's the old check is in the mail trick, isn't it?" But I could tell that she wasn't joking. Up until now I had been pleased with her course, but I was upset that she didn't believe I had mailed the money.

She did get the check that day and thanked me that evening. But what would have happened if she had called me and I just didn't happen to have $150 lying around the office? Would it have been fair to blame me because I was unprepared to pay? This was an advertising course, not a mind-reading course.

The instructor got her $50 deposit in advance because she demanded it in advance. If she had told me she had to have payment in full at the first class meeting, I would have brought her the money then. I would have thought that I had no other choice.

Salespeople are often reluctant to discuss financial arrangements with a customer for fear of losing a sale. You can understand their fear, but isn't their apprehension irrational? The customer knows he's going to have to pay for the goods or services sooner or later. Don't you think it would be nicer to let the customer know when he is supposed to pay?

Many collection problems would disappear if someone would just tell the customer in advance when and how much he is expected to pay. Most people would play by the rules if they only knew them.

### Nice Courtesy Call

Making a courtesy call to your customer shortly after he makes his purchase is probably one of the smartest things you can do. Before the first payment is due, call the customer and thank him for his business and make sure he is satisfied. Very few companies go to this much trouble, even though customers appreciate this personal attention. This attentiveness sets you apart from the ordinary business and shows that you care.

There is another benefit to this call. You now have the opportunity to review the payment arrangements with your customer again. That way, in case your salesperson forgot to discuss the financial details, you still have a chance before the payment is due to explain your expectations.

Then, if the customer doesn't pay on the scheduled due date, you have effectively eliminated the excuse that he didn't know when to pay. He also will be less likely to say he didn't pay because he found a defect in your product or service since he had an opportunity to tell you at the time of your courtesy call. If he does, however, have a legitimate complaint at the time of your courtesy call, you can resolve his problem solved before the scheduled payment date and still receive your payment on time.

A retail store owner who was attending one of our collection seminars responded to our nice courtesy call suggestion by saying he would never do this. He said that this would increase his number of complaints too much. I'm sure you'll agree that this merchant is much better off if he knows about his customers' problems so that he can solve them. His customers will pay better and they will continue to do business with him longer.

We have a client who is a carpet dealer. It is the responsibility of his customer service employee to call each customer after installation to verify customer satisfaction and to review payment arrangements. I visited ABC Carpet one day and listened to one of their nice courtesy calls:

**ABC Carpet:**  Mr. Jones?

**Jones:**  Yes . . .

**ABC:**  I'm Mr. Smith with ABC and I was calling to thank you for your business and make sure you are satisfied with the carpet that our men installed Friday.

**Jones:**  Oh yes. Your men did a fine job. I was particularly impressed with the way they cleaned up after they finished.

**ABC:**  You made a smart decision to buy #235 Acme carpeting. We've installed thousands of yards of this quality product in high-traffic areas and our customers are always happy with its performance. By the way, did our salesman, Mr. Jackson, mention that if you pay for your carpet before July 10th, you can deduct an extra 2 percent? That would save you $60.

**Jones:**  Mr. Jackson did tell me, but I told him that I needed the full thirty days to pay.

**ABC:**  That's fine—the option's yours. I'll put it in the computer that you'll pay your $3,000 balance by July 30th. I want to thank you again for your business and if there is anything I can do for you please give me a call.

Look what ABC accomplished with this one telephone call:

- It showed the customer that the company cared.
- It verified the level of service of the installers, which is good quality control.
- It verified that the salesperson reviewed the financial arrangements with the customer.
- It gave the company another opportunity to explain its payment expectations—eliminating the excuse that "I didn't know when I was supposed to pay."
- It positively reinforced the sale and made the customer feel good about himself for making such a smart purchase.
- It gave the company a chance to find out about a complaint early enough to solve it so that payment could be made on time.
- It distinguished the company from the competition.

Here's another real-life example from Martin:

There is only one company that I do business with that always makes a courtesy call. The service department of a local Honda dealership always calls me after I have my car serviced.

A few months ago the service department did some work on my car and I was billed a good bit more than I expected. I complained to the service manager, but he was defensive and gave me no satisfaction. Sure enough, a few days later I was called by the customer service representative. I shared with her my dissatisfaction, and within the hour the service manager called me back. This time he offered me a compensating discount on my next service and I have continued to do business with him.

If no one had made a "nice courtesy call," I would have probably changed to another dealership or mechanic.

## Urgent First Payment

If you want to have a greater chance of building a healthier and more trustworthy relationship with your customers and to ensure getting them to pay on time, you must make sure they make their first payment on time. From the very beginning, make it absolutely clear to your customers what your requirements and expectations are and that they understand that not paying on time has its consequences.

At Mr. King Furniture, if a customer misses his first payment, there is a 19 percent chance that he will pay as agreed. If he makes his first payment on time, there's a 75 percent chance he will pay as agreed. When a Mr. King customer misses his first payment, we are quick to follow up.

Most of you are dealing with customers or clients with a better credit profile than our customers, but we caution you that the first payment is the most critical. This is the first chance your customer has to prove his credit worthiness, and it does not bode well when he doesn't follow through on his first commitment.

When we did our statistical analysis to establish our credit-scoring criteria for Mr. King Furniture, we found that the most important variable in predicting future payment was whether the customer made his first payment on time. Unfortunately we don't know whether the customer is going to miss his first payment until after we make the sale.

You want your customers to know that not paying on time has its consequences. When you allow your debtors to do what they want, you are implicitly consenting to their behavior. By letting them run late on their first payment, you have set a precedent for all future payments. If they pay late the first time and you don't react, they have learned a very valuable lesson. They have learned that if they pay late, nothing will happen. If, however, they discover that you react negatively when they don't pay the first time, they will assume that you will always react negatively and act accordingly.

Here's the bottom line: You can train your customers to pay on your payment plan or they will train you to pay on theirs.

## Exceptional Service

Chapter 5 covers why it's in your best interest to provide exceptional service. Most of the time, if you provide exceptional service in addition to following the preceding steps, your customers will only want to do business with you and they will pay as promised.

Sometimes, however, you walk down the "avenue" perfectly and your customers still don't pay. What do you do? Write them letters? Visit them personally? Phone? Find out in the following chapters.

# Ease, Effectiveness, and Practicality

*If you think no one cares if you're dead or alive,*
*try not paying your bills.*
*—Anonymous*

## Collection Letters: The Least Effective and Most Used Collection Method

The story is told of a man who one night is on his hands and knees searching for something on a street corner. A bystander asks if he can help. The man explains that he's dropped his watch and can't find it. The two of them stoop down and look for the watch until finally the bystander becomes frustrated and asks the man where exactly he lost it. The man replies that he dropped it across the street, but since there was more light under the street lamp, he was looking there.

We are reminded of this story every time we hear about collectors who continue to send collection mail even after it's obvious that additional letters aren't going to be effective. If two or three letters don't work, why should

four, five, or six be successful? There is no problem with
collection letters per se; the problem is too many collection
letters.

We were once hired by a business owner who was having major accounts receivable problems. We met with the
owner, comptroller, and credit manager. The comptroller
complained that his average days outstanding was growing
monthly and he was becoming increasingly concerned.

We asked the credit manager how he handled his delinquent accounts. He said that when a bill reached thirty
days past due, his computer automatically sent out a past
due statement. Then an additional statement was sent each
month for five more months. If there were still no payment, the credit manager reviewed each account and then
sent two personal letters demanding payment.

The account was then turned over to a letter service
(a collection agency that only sends collection mail). A series of five additional letters was generated. This means
that the debtor was sent thirteen collection notices over a
period of about a year. It's no wonder that the company
had collection difficulties.

It's true that sending collection mail is quick and easy.
And, even better, you don't have to confront your debtor.
But it buys the debtor time and we all know by now that
time is the weapon of the debtor. Collection letters also
have some other serious shortcomings:

- Collection mail is only a one-way communication.
- You don't know if the debtor got the letter.
- You don't know the debtor's reaction.
  Does she plan to pay?
  Does she plan to not pay?
  Was she satisfied with your product or service?
  Does she intend to sue you if you pursue collection?
- Letters can only attempt to motivate a customer to

pay her debt; they usually don't uncover reasons for nonpayment.

Collection mail can play a major role in your collection process. By sending letters you avoid more time-consuming and expensive methods. The secret, however, is to know when to quit and try something else.

## Suggestions for Collection Letters

Bill-collection agencies in England began lacing their invoices with a product containing androsterone, a chemical secreted from men's armpits and groins that is known to be a sex attractant in some species. In one preliminary study, mailed invoices treated with the product resulted in a 14 percent higher payment rate than untreated bills. (*Health Magazine*, January/February, 1993)

You may feel uncomfortable with such a collection mail technique, so here are some other ideas:

- Shorten your series to two or three letters.
- Send letters out ten to fourteen days apart rather than thirty days apart.
- Distinguish the envelopes used for successive mailings:
  Use different colors and sizes. Pink or red are the most effective colors. (Many debtors wait until the envelope turns red—so start off with red.)
  Change styles frequently.
  Hand write.
  Don't put your name on the envelope.
  Write on the outside of the envelope. (Example: "Personal and Confidential")

Use "Address Correction Requested."
* Compose the letters carefully:
  Make them short and simple.
  Set a deadline for the debtor.
  Clearly state the consequences for acting or not act-
    ing as requested.
  Escalate your demands in succeeding letters.
  Underscore words or sentences you want to empha-
    size or type in boldface.
  Include a P.S. (postscript) to increase response.
* Include a return postage-paid envelope.

Figure 2 is the "world's shortest collection letter," suggested to us by Michael Kahn of Interregional Credit Systems of Minneapolis. It often is effective for those
situations in which promises are made and not kept. It also
fits well with the "shorter the better" approach to writing
collection letters.

## Figure 2    The "world's shortest collection letter."

*Date*

John Smith
ABC Industries
100 Main Street
Anywhere, US 00000


Dear Mr. Smith:


**WELL?**


Sincerely,


David Sher
AmSher Collection Services

Figure 3 is a letter that was recommended to us by a participant in one of our seminars. She said that it's very effective when you want to send one last letter before you turn an account over to a third party for collection.

## Figure 3 Letter of last resort.

*Date*

John Smith
ABC Industries
100 Main Street
Anywhere, USA 00000


Dear Mr. Smith:

We hate Collection Agencies.

No, we're not being sarcastic. They cost us money, hurt the customer's credit standing, and give people the idea that we're against them.

We want to do what we can to help you, but at this point our choices are being limited since you won't respond to the numerous statements we sent to you.

Please call toll free at 1-800-555-5555 and let us help or send payment within the next seven (7) days.

You'll find we're still willing to help. We don't want to send this to collection.

Sincerely,


Martin Sher
ACME Products, Inc.

## The Personal Visit: The Most Effective and Least Used Collection Method

Most people would prefer not to confront their debtors face-to-face. However, as Martin demonstrates by the following story, it is the most effective method of collection.

> I received a frantic call from a business friend of mine. One of her customers was several weeks past due on a bill for $80,000, and she didn't know what to do. Her debtor was located nearby, so I suggested that she go see him in person. She reported back to me a couple of days later.
>
> The customer was surprised to see her, but was very nice. He bragged about how his business had grown and took her on a tour of his factory. He explained that his fast growth had caused him to be short of cash, but promised to mail her a check within a week or two.
>
> I recommended she make a follow-up note for two weeks later, and if he didn't pay as promised, she should go back and see him again. She groaned, but said she would.
>
> She called me a few weeks later and was as excited as if she had won the lottery. In a sense she had. He didn't pay as he had agreed, but she followed my advice and went back to see him. He wrote her a check for the full amount on the spot. Was it worth $80,000 to personally visit the man? You bet it was.

Sometimes it's best to surprise your debtor. Other times you might want to call in advance. If you are unable to contact your debtor ahead of time, you might consider leaving a message specifying the date and time you will visit. Make sure you bring all the proper documentation with you so you can prove exactly how much is owed.

We asked the executive director of a local charity that raises a lot of money to rate the different ways he solicits funds. He said that by far his most effective method is to have solicitors meet face-to-face with their prospects. Telephone solicitation is second. Mail campaigns are third. This professional fund-raiser could just as easily have been talking about collecting past due accounts. Because personal visits are often impractical and expensive, and mailing is your least effective alternative, the telephone is usually your most practical and efficient option.

Telephone collections are covered thoroughly in Chapters 12, 13, and 14, but we want to leave you here with the story of an unconventional technique used by a client of ours. He owns a photographic and printing company, and he had a customer who was several months past due. After writing and getting no response, he called, but could not get the customer to come to the phone or return his calls. Finally, he went to the customer's office, but the gentleman refused to see him.

In desperation and frustration our client went back to his office and had a sign printed in big red bold letters that screamed: I COLLECT BAD DEBTS. Then he returned to his customer's busy waiting room, placed the sign across his lap for everyone to see, and waited.

He collected his money.

[Author's note: We would definitely *not* recommend this aggressive collection technique.]

# Why People Don't Call

*A woman complained that she was receiving panting phone calls. The police visited the caller's house. The family dog had mastered the trick of knocking the receiver off the hook and pawing the redial button.*
—The Economist

## Dialing for $$$, Part One

Martin walked into the barbershop a couple of days before one of our collection seminars and found that he had become a big celebrity. His picture had just appeared in *The Birmingham News* announcing the seminar and everyone wanted to talk about how to collect money. The barber proudly stated that he never had any trouble getting paid. He said, "I always ask for my money."

Such a statement doesn't sound very profound, but you would be amazed how many people overlook the obvious. Your most practical, effective, and efficient option is to telephone and ask for your money. As discussed in Chapter 11, you would get your best results if you could go see every single person face-to-face, but if your debtor lives far away or if there are a lot of debtors to collect from, then your only practical choice is to use the telephone. However, even though using the telephone is vastly more effective than letters, many people hesitate to pick up the phone and make that important call.

Because most business offices aren't large enough to have a collection department, an employee is usually given the responsibility to make collection calls along with his or her other duties. The employee is generally not trained in collections and is supposed to do collection work in between other jobs. This arrangement rarely works effectively.

If you could be a fly on the wall in the typical office and could see what was going on below, you would understand. Employees almost always prioritize their jobs so that they do everything else first and do their collection work last. They do their paperwork. They clean up their desks. They offer to help others. They send out mail. They do anything and everything else. If any time is left, they will make a collection call.

Even our own government poorly utilizes the telephone for collections. In a July 6, 1991, article published in *The Birmingham News,* by Newhouse News Service, titled "IRS Urged to Accelerate Calls to Delinquent Taxpayers," it says: "Calls are not being made to taxpayers when they are likely to be home. . . . Call site employees spent 52 percent of their time on leave, in training, managing or working on administrative matters rather than working on collecting delinquent taxes."

These circumstances are typical of many offices. Every other job gets done except collections. Occasionally, you will run across someone who makes calling a priority and that person is usually the boss, the spouse of the boss, or someone with some collection experience or knowledge. Otherwise, telephone collection effort is haphazard.

Why don't people ask for their money? Almost everyone agrees that if you want to collect the most money as fast as you can, then you have to ask. Why then do most employees procrastinate? We've found four major reasons why people won't pick up the phone and call:

1. They are afraid of the debtor's reaction.
2. They feel sorry for the debtor.
3. They are afraid they don't know the collection laws and will do something illegal.
4. They don't know what to say.

Let's examine each of these excuses.

## Fear of the Debtor's Reaction

This is an actual letter we received from a debtor

Dear Mr. King,

I'm writing to let you know that I have been in prison over the last eight (8) months. A person broke into my apartment and stole everything. I found the person who did it and shot him four (4) times. I will take up my account as soon as I am released from prison.

Very truly yours,

John Doe
P.S. I just got your address four (4) days ago.

Would you like to be the one to call this debtor when he is released from jail?

Even if your debtor isn't a convict, many people don't want to call for payment because they are afraid of the debtor's reaction. And, it's true, many debtors do react negatively when you call them for any one or several of the following reasons:

• Your call may be an interruption. Your debtor may be busy doing something else and your call may be an ill-timed disturbance. He may be trying to beat a deadline at work. He may be in a meeting. He may be eating dinner with his family or at the climax of a great television movie. You have called at your convenience—not his.

• You may have caught your debtor by surprise. You have had a chance to plan your call. You have thought about what you are going to say and are prepared for the conversation. Your debtor, on the other hand, may be caught off guard and act badly.

• He may be anxious about his situation. There has probably been some event in your debtor's life that has caused him not to pay. This troublesome situation may cause him to be apprehensive and say the wrong thing.

• He may feel guilty over his nonpayment. Most people intend to pay their bills, so they may feel ashamed when they don't pay. They may take out their embarrassment on you.

• He may be unhappy about parting with his money. When your debtor picks up the receiver and finds someone at the other end who wants to take his money away, he may make some unkind comments to the caller.

Being prepared for the probable reaction of your debtors and understanding where it's coming from will help allay your fears about calling. (See Chapter 13 for additional discussion of precall preparations, including how to deal with debtors' reactions.)

## Sympathy for the Debtor

"I don't have any money." "I'm short of cash." "I just can't afford to pay today." These are typical debtor responses. And since all of us have had financial problems at one time or another, we might feel badly for the debtor. We are just like the people we are calling. We have problems and they have problems. It's easy to feel sorry for them.

There are many honest debtors conscientiously working through their financial problems. There is also a group of debtors whom we will call "credit criminals" who run up large bills and have no intention of paying.

Similarly, there was a story in *The Wall Street Journal* about the Girl Scouts in central North Carolina. Each year their Council has to deal with a sizable number of people who write bad checks when paying for cookies. "The bouncing pieces of paper have ranged from $2.50 to $1,100—totaling $50,000." Can you believe that there are people who would write bad checks to Girl Scouts? It's hard to feel sorry for anyone trying to cheat little girls.

How good an excuse is it for someone to tell you that they don't have any money? Let's assume you are trying to collect from a business. You call up and ask for the payment that is long overdue. They tell you that the company is having terrible cash flow problems and just doesn't have the cash to pay. Now let's think rationally about this statement. "I don't have any money to pay my bills." Let's see. You called them on the phone and they answered, so they must be paying their phone bill. You called them at some location, so they must be paying their rent. When you called, a live human being answered the phone, so they must be paying some salaries. You know what? We'll bet you that the lights are on and the heat or air-conditioning is running. So even the power company is being paid. We'll also bet you that in addition to the phone company, the employees, the landlord, and the power company that there are other bills being paid. So in order to make your debtor's statement more accurate, we need to rephrase it from "I don't have money to pay my bills," to "I don't have money to pay *you*."

But what if your debtor is an individual and not a company, and she tells you that she doesn't have any money to pay? She had to have a telephone in order to answer your call. She had to have a place of residence. The lights and other utilities were probably on. She probably has food to eat. So she's obviously paying some of her bills. She just prioritized her debts and you didn't make her list.

Doctors tell us they are the last to be paid. Cable companies tell us they are the last to be paid. Furniture retailers tell us they are the last to be paid. Everyone can't be last! Your debtor has decided which bills are important and which ones aren't. Obviously, your debt isn't that important. So is your sympathy for your debtor justified?

Almost everyone can come up with money when properly motivated. For example, let's assume today is Wednesday. Payday is not until Friday. You get a call from one of your creditors demanding a payment of $200 by 5 P.M. tomorrow. You explain that you are unable to pay until Friday.

Now let us tell you about a friend of ours. He's very wealthy and very eccentric. How wealthy is he? He loves expensive automobiles and he buys a new luxury car every two or three months. How eccentric is he? He gets some kind of perverse pleasure from selling these almost new cars to complete strangers for (you guessed it) $200 each.

Yesterday he called and asked us to find someone to

buy the Mercedes he's currently driving. David volunteered to be the purchaser, but, unfortunately, he will only sell to complete strangers. We figure we should reward someone who has helped us, and since you helped us financially by buying this book, suppose we call and offer to sell the car to you on the condition that you come up with the money by 5 P.M. tomorrow. We bet you will find a way to come up with the money. It's all a matter of priorities.

## Ignorance of Collection Laws

*The Evans Mortuary in Richmond, Texas, dumped the body of a dead man on his son's doorstep when the son was unable to pay the full price of cremation.*
—Health Magazine, January/February 1993

The principal federal law covering consumer collection activity is Public Law 95-109, commonly known as the Fair Debt Collection Practices Act (FDCPA). (State laws may vary.) Keep in mind that commercial or business-to-business collections are excluded. This rather detailed law contains eighteen sections and was passed to regulate debt collections by collection agencies and collection attorneys. If you are doing consumer collection work for other businesses, it is imperative that you become familiar with this important piece of legislation. If you are doing collection work for your own company, you are not specifically covered by this act, but I strongly recommend that you follow its rules. The provisions of the law are fair and reasonable. Its objective is to avoid situations like the following incident where, apparently, threats were being made to clients of phone-sex lines by a collection agency that specialized in this type of debt collection. They extorted more than $2 million by saying they would inform the clients' spouses and employers if they didn't take care of their debts to the sex lines. It's because of unscrupulous activity like this that the FDCPA was passed. You can't lie to a debtor. You can't threaten illegal acts. You can't make false threats.

Debtors continually warn our collectors that it's against the law to threaten them. This is not true. There's no provision in the law that prevents a creditor from threatening a debtor. But you cannot threaten *an illegal act* and your intent must be to actually *follow through* on your threat.

You can't threaten to break someone's arms or legs. You can't threaten to kidnap someone's children. You can't threaten to break down a door or have someone thrown in jail. These are all illegal acts.

But you can threaten a legal act as long as you intend to follow through with the threatened action. Don't threaten to sue within five days unless you plan to do so. Don't threaten to attach your debtor's property by Thursday unless that is what you are going to do. Even if the FDCPA had never been written, it is important to remember from a business standpoint, you are better off if you always follow through on your threats. If you don't and your debtor doesn't pay, he sure won't believe you the next time you threaten him.

We have a cardinal rule in our business. If we make a commitment to a customer, we always fulfill that commitment. We always do what we say we're going to do whether it is good or bad. In our retail furniture store, if we promise a customer that we will be out to his house by 3 P.M. Thursday, to fix his television, then we're there by 3 P.M. And if we promise her that if she doesn't pay her bill by noon on Friday we will repossess her washer, then we fulfill that commitment as well.

You might be asking, "Do you always have to follow through on every threat every time to stay out of trouble?"

We recommend that your intent should be to follow through.

Our collectors are also regularly warned by our debtors that it's against the law to harass them. They are right. It is against the law to harass them, but what does the word "harass" mean? If we call debtors and they promise to pay on Monday, and don't pay, and we call them on Tuesday, are we harassing them? If they then promise to pay Thursday and don't pay, and we call them on Friday, are we harassing them? We think it is safe to say that we are not. But if we call them on Monday and they promise to pay on Friday and then we call them Tuesday, Wednesday, and Thursday before the payment is due, we are harassing them and are probably breaking the law.

Other provisions of the act prevent you from calling before 8 A.M. or after 9 P.M. The law will not allow you to ring your debtor's phone continuously, and you cannot use obscene language. You also cannot discuss the bill with anyone other than a spouse unless the debtor tells you to talk to his designated attorney. The law is rather lengthy, but if you'll just be honest with your debtor and use common sense, you will stay out of trouble.

A participant at one of our seminars was telling us about a business client she was trying to collect from. She said she had talked to the bookkeeper and the comptroller and still hadn't received payment. Finally she decided it was time to talk to the owner. She called him day after day, but the owner was never available and would not return her calls. So, in desperation, she finally called the owner, and when asked the nature of her call, responded that she was his wife. Sure enough, the call was put through. But as soon as the debtor realized that he had been fooled, he slammed the phone down. She didn't accomplish anything.

In another example, Art Buchwald, the famous columnist, has some unconventional ideas on how to get a protective secretary to put a call through to her boss. He suggests that you tell the secretary, "We just got Mr. Golson's test back from the lab." And if that doesn't work, he proposes that you tell the secretary, "I just found Mr. Golson's American Express Card on the water bed at the Silk Pussy Cat Motel. Does he want me to bring it in or should I mail it to him?"

Fraudulent and dishonest tactics don't work. Not only are they ineffective, but they often make it more difficult to collect.

At a recent collectors' convention we attended, one of the collection agency owners was bragging about how he had collected an account from a famous "rock star." A public relations company had done some work for this well-known celebrity and had not been paid. The celebrity probably didn't even know about the delinquency because matters like this are generally handled by a business manager or agent. But in any event, the account was turned over to the previously mentioned collector.

This clever debt collector called the business manager pretending to be a freelance reporter for *The National Enquirer.* He said he had heard that the celebrity was a deadbeat who didn't pay his bills and he was getting ready to publish a story about him. He was just waiting for the pending lawsuit to be filed. According to the collector this potential negative publicity scared the business manager into immediately paying the debt.

You might say that this example proves that duplicity pays off. I don't believe it does. From a legal standpoint, the collector did nothing illegal because the FDCPA does not apply to commercial collections. And even if his act were illegal, people break the law every day and don't get caught. That doesn't make it right.

We don't believe that it is in your best interest to collect in an unethical manner. Even if you do collect some money on occasion by stretching the truth, your reputation is damaged.

Just ask yourself if what you are about to do seems honest and moral. If it is, then you are more than likely not breaking the law. So you needn't be afraid of not knowing the details of collection laws.

# Before You Make That Call

*I have an answering machine in my car. It says, "I'm home now, but leave me a message and I'll call when I'm out."*
—*Anonymous*

## Dialing for $$$, Part Two

No collection call is a welcome call. Never have we heard a debtor exclaim, "Hallelujah! It's the bill collector!" So even if you aren't afraid of the debtor's reaction, don't feel sorry for the debtor, know the collection laws, and know exactly what to say, how do you deal with the rejection?

We're reminded of a story told by a friend and client, Gene Smith, who is currently in the finance business, but in an earlier life had been a firefighter. Gene tells of a door-to-door salesman who stopped by the fire department to get a drink of water. Gene asked him what motivated him to keep knocking on doors when most people rejected him.

The salesman, who was obviously very methodical, kept detailed records. He said he totaled his profit from last year and divided that figure by the number of houses he visited. He calculated that he earned $10 every time he knocked on a door—a pretty good incentive to keep knocking.

The same is true with telephone collections. Not everyone will pay, but how much you ultimately collect will be determined by how many calls you make. But before you pick up the telephone, you need to be prepared mentally and emotionally.

## Be Ready for the Reaction

Let's say you get married. Just like Cinderella and the handsome prince, you plan on living happily ever after. Well one day, the stork drops by and leaves you a howling, screaming, demanding infant. You love this baby. You sing to her. You play with her. You feed her and give her baths. How does this bundle of joy treat you? She wakes you up in the middle of the night. She makes messes in her diaper. She throws up. How do you deal with this emotionally? Well, you certainly don't take your baby's actions personally. Your baby is not trying to get even with you (though sometimes the thought may cross your mind).

Infants sometimes don't sleep through the night. Infants are not housebroken. Infants occasionally get sick. A mother once said that you spend the first eighteen months of a baby's life teaching him to walk and talk and the rest of his childhood telling him to shut up and sit down. This is just what you expect from babies and children.

When you call a debtor and she reacts badly, she is not attacking you personally. She isn't out to get you. In most cases, she doesn't even know who you are. So there is no reason for you to feel poorly about yourself or lower your self-esteem. Babies scream and cry—debtors scream and cry. There is sometimes very little difference.

Let's look at another example. You've been reading for a while and it's time to take a break. You have some chores to do, so you close your book and walk outside to your car.

All of a sudden a rain cloud appears overhead and it dumps a boatload of water on you—soaking you from head to toe. You might not like being wet and you may get angry and upset, but would you feel that the cloud had it in for you personally? No, Mr. Rain Cloud was not out to get you. You understand that you are dealing with the laws of nature and gravity. You expect that if you get under enough rain clouds that sooner or later you're going to get wet. It's just one of those many risks you face in life. You should also know that if you call enough debtors, sooner or later one of them is going to get angry and dump on you. The debtor has nothing personal against you, so don't take it personally.

## Understand the Power of Persuasion

You're prepared for the debtor's reaction. You're not going to feel sorry for the debtor. And you feel comfortable that you're not going to break the law. You pick up the receiver and dial . . .

**Debtor:** Hello

**You:** ?????

Uh oh! You don't know what to say! It's difficult to know what to say to a debtor—isn't it? You're probably supposed to tell your debtor that she must make her payment by 5 o'clock or else. Or else what?

Before you answer that question, let us relate one of our favorite Aesop's Fables, "The Wind and the Sun":

The Wind was self-centered and stuck-up. He walked around the sky bragging about how great he was. He said, "I am the Wind—no one is greater than I."

No one would stand up to the Wind because everyone was afraid of his mean and very loud manner. Then one day the Sun could stand it no longer and said, "Wind, I am sick and tired of you going around bragging about yourself and I want you to stop."

The Wind replied, "All right, Sun, you think you're so great—I'll make you a bet that will prove that I am greater than you."

The Sun thought for a minute and then replied, "Okay, I'm sick and tired of your bragging—what do you propose?"

The Wind answered, "Look at that man walking along the road. I can get his coat off more quickly than you can." The Sun replied, "We will see about that. I will let you try first."

So the Wind tried to make the man take off his coat. He blew and blew. But the man only pulled his coat more closely around himself. The Wind blew harder and harder. But the harder he blew, the tighter the man held onto his coat. Finally the Wind said, "I give up. I cannot get his coat off."

It was now the Sun's turn. He shone as hard as he could. As the man got warmer and warmer, he loosened up his coat and finally he became so hot, he took it off.

As you get ready to pick up the phone to make your collection calls, remember the moral of this story: When you tell someone that they have to do something, they usually try to prove to you that they don't have to do anything that they don't want to do.

You're much better off if you can persuade the person that he or she *wants* to do something. This is certainly true in collections where there are generally two types of collectors. To be consistent, the first type of collector we call the WIND and the other we call the SUN. The WIND calls the debtor and says something like this:

> **The WIND:** Mr. Debtor, I am John Wind from Wind Collection Services. You owe a past due bill to Acme Co.
>
> **The debtor:** But . . .
>
> **The WIND:** I don't want to hear any buts . . . I want you to pay it now!!!

The WIND demands payment from everyone. He treats everyone the same and he never listens to the debtor. He figures simply that if he makes enough calls, someone is bound to pay.

The SUN, on the other hand, understands that he has a better chance of being successful if he can prove to the debtor that it is in the debtor's best interest to pay. He actively listens to the debtor, convinces the debtor that he is on her side, and works with the debtor to help her find a way to pay.

## You Must Remember This

Finally, keep in mind three special keys to successful collection calls:

1. Focusing on a goal
2. Having an assumptive attitude
3. Maintaining control of the conversation

• The Collector's Goal. The collector's goal should be *to get payment in full on the first contact.* This is critical. If you want to collect the most money as fast as you can, net of expenses, then there is no sense in having to call the debtor over and over again to get your money. Just make one call and do what it takes to get it over with once and for all. It's faster and cheaper that way.

• The Assumptive Attitude. As discussed in the "Attitude" section, it's important to have an assumptive attitude when you collect: You must assume that you are going to be successful every time. In addition, before you make a collection call, you should always make two assumptions:

1. The debtor owes the debt.
2. The debtor will pay the debt.

Without an assumptive attitude, you are doomed to failure. If you are not totally convinced that your debtor will pay, you don't stand much of a chance making the collection.

• Maintaining Control of the Conversation. As warned in Chapter 12, when you make a collection call, you're at risk that the debtor may react negatively. It's easy to get upset and get down to the debtor's level, but this response never works. If the debtor screams and you start screaming, you are finished. First, you will never win the debtor over to your side by raising your voice. And, second, it is very easy for the debtor to get rid of you. All she has to do is hang up. If you have acted inappropriately, the debtor will avoid talking to you in the future. You are much better off treating the debtor with respect so that she will be willing to talk to you again.

But how do you handle the debtor who loses control and raises her voice? The louder your debtor talks, the softer you should talk. The worse your debtor acts, the nicer you should become. If you can stay on the line long enough, you will find that the debtor often will become embarrassed about her behavior and try to prove to you that she's not such a shrew.

**14**

# Blueprint of a
# Successful Telephone
# Collection Call

## Dialing for $$$, Part Three

According to the American Collectors Association, there are eight steps to a successful telephone collection call:

1. Identify the debtor.
2. Identify yourself.
3. Ask for payment in full.
4. Pause and listen.
5. Determine the problem.
6. Find a solution.
7. Close the deal.
8. Document your collection effort.

Don't panic! This is really a very simple process. As you'll see, these steps make logical sense and flow easily from one to the other.

## Step 1, Identify the Debtor

You want to be certain that the person you are talking with is the correct debtor. According to the Fair Debt Collection Practices Act (FDCPA), it is illegal to talk to anyone about a debt except the debtor, the debtor's spouse, or the debtor's attorney. Let's see what can go wrong:

Phone rings . . .

**Debtor:** Hello . . .

**You:** Jim Smith?

**Debtor:** Yes . . .

**You:** I am Martin Sher from Mr. King Furniture. Your account is seriously delinquent, Mr. Smith, and must be paid now. Will . . . [debtor interrupts]

**Debtor:** I don't know what you're talking about! I'm 63 years old and I haven't bought any furniture in 20 years . . .

**You:** You bought a table from us on June 6th . . .

**Debtor:** I did no such thing—that must have been my son Jim, Jr.,—you dimwit!

Oops! That's not what's supposed to happen. Obviously, we have mixed up a senior and a junior.

You also may have a problem with people with common names. Take the name Jim Smith, as used in our example. There is no telling how many Jim Smiths there are in the world. In fact, we understand that there is a national convention each year for people named Jim Smith, and literally hundreds of Jim Smiths attend.

It's easy to see how you can have a problem with a

k-up with a less com-
on a television news-
e in the United States
hat one of them lives
treet. We don't know
try to collect from the

ig to the right debtor
it sounds. One of our
she called the home of
one and the collector
ginning with "identify-
e debtor realized that
this was a collection call, s.... upted and said that she was sorry, but she was not Mary Jones. Our collection then asked her who she was. She replied, "I'm my daughter."

When you are making a commercial or business-to-business collection call, the difficulty becomes identifying and trying to speak with the person who has the authority to issue payment. A great deal of time can be wasted attempting to talk with the wrong person. If requesting payment from the accounts payable clerk doesn't get you your money, don't be shy about moving up the organization. Ask for the comptroller, the president, the chief executive officer, or the owner.

It can sometimes be a challenge to get the top executive on the phone. If you have a problem, we recommend that you try to call his or her office before 8 A.M., during lunch hours, or after 5 P.M., when the secretary may not be around to intercept the call. (Since this is a commercial collection and you are calling a business, you are not limited by law to calling after 8 in the morning or before 9 at night. However, check your state law to see whether it supersedes federal law.)

## Step 2, Identify Yourself

Tell the debtor your name and what company you represent.

## Step 3, Ask for Payment in Full

If you are new at collecting, we recommend that you write a short script to help you with this portion of the call. That way, after you've identified the debtor and identified yourself, you can just read a few short lines. Figure 4 is a sample script that you might use. You may have to make some minor adjustments to suit your situation.

Figure 4   Sample script for requesting payment in full.

> "Your account is seriously delinquent Mr./Ms. _____ and must be paid now. Will you be in our office today to pay this account in full, or would you prefer to send us a check today for $____ [full amount] so that we can clear this up?"

Notice that you give your debtor two options that are both acceptable: Can he or she come in today to pay or mail a check today? You don't want to leave it to the debtor to suggest his or her own payment plan. Don't say:

> "Your account is seriously delinquent Mr./Ms. _____. How do you want to pay?"

By specifying your debtor's options you have a better chance of getting what you want.

## Step 4, Pause and Listen

You may worry that after you complete steps one, two, and three and then pause to listen to your debtor's response that he or she won't say anything. We can assure you this won't happen. The debtor always has something to say. Your only problem may be that your debtor has too much to say and you lose control of the conversation. Silence makes people uncomfortable and they rush to fill it, giving you the opportunity to hear your debtor's reason for not paying.

You may think that this "pause and listen" step is the easiest of the eight steps because you don't have to say anything. The truth is that this fourth step is the most demanding and also the most important. It's true that you don't have to say anything, but you do have to listen, and listening can be very difficult. If you don't listen, however, you don't have much chance of understanding your debtor's problem and finding a payment solution.

Remember the difference between the SUN and the WIND. The WIND treats all debtors the same. The SUN responds to each debtor individually. How does the SUN know how to respond to each debtor? The answer is by listening carefully and searching for clues for a way to work with the debtor to help him or her figure out a way to pay.

## Step 5, Determine the Problem

Once you've made your request for payment, your debtor will probably respond in one of four ways by

1. promising to pay
2. telling you that he or she has no intention of paying
3. disputing the debt
4. objecting or stalling

If he or she promises to pay, great! Mission accomplished. Otherwise, you should try to determine your debtor's intent to pay just as soon as possible. It's a dead giveaway when your debtor says, "I'm just not going to pay." Or, he tells you to, "Get lost." Or she says, "Why don't you go ahead and sue me?"

It's not quite so simple when he or she uses a more indirect approach, such as breaking promises or just not returning phone calls. But the message is the same: "I'm not going to pay!"

If your debtor cannot pay the full balance now, try to get him or her to send you postdated checks. The first check should be sent and dated immediately. That way you can determine your debtor's intentions without having to wait. Some creditors don't like to accept postdated checks because they fear that some will bounce. But we've found that most of the time the checks are good. We recommend that you call or write the debtor before depositing. (Third-party collectors are required by the FDCPA to notify the debtor.)

Once you've determined that your debtor has no intention of paying, then you have two options. You can turn the account over to a third party for collection (see Chapters 16 and 17) or you can discontinue all collection efforts and file the account away. Don't continue to waste time on this debt unless you're a masochist or unless you have nothing better to do with your time.

If your debtor disputes the bill, then you need to determine as quickly as possible whether the complaint is legitimate. Naturally, if your debtor has a valid complaint, you'll want to get it resolved as quickly as possible. If the complaint is not legitimate, your debtor is either stalling or telling you he or she is not going to pay.

At Mr. King Furniture we attempt to call every customer twice before the first payment is due. The first call is placed two or three days after delivery to make sure our customer is satisfied. ("nice courtesy call"). Then we call back a few days before the customer's due date to verify customer satisfaction and to reemphasize the importance of the first payment. ("nice courtesy call" number 2). These calls are not collection calls. We just want to make sure that we've satisfied all complaints before the first payment is due and verify that that our customer understands the payment arrangements.

When your debtor makes an objection, listen closely. He or she is trying to tell you the reason for nonpayment. You should try to determine the real problem and find a solution.

The most common debtor stall is the debtor pleading a lack of money. He or she may say:

- Our company is having some cash-flow problems.
- My boss cut back my hours, and I'm not making as much money.
- My wife is in the hospital, and I've had some unbelievable medical bills.
- I've lost my job and don't know how I will be able to pay.

The message is the same: "I don't have the money and I don't know how I am going to pay." Your job is to help your debtor find a way to pay.

## Step 6, Find a Solution

If you've listened carefully to your debtor, you should be able to work with him or her to find a solution. Try to avoid creating an adversarial relationship. You want to work to-gether as a team to find a way to get the bill paid.

Let's assume that you are trying to collect from a busi-ness and the owner tells you he is short of cash. You might suggest that he get money from one or more of the follow-ing sources:

- Personal charge card
- Bank loan
- Increasing an existing loan
- Checking or savings account
- Credit union
- Finance company
- Consolidation loan
- Relatives—spouse, parents, grandparents, etc.
- Employees
- Borrowing from life insurance
- Canceling insurance
- Mortgage home
- Second mortgage home
- Selling assets
- Rental income
- Tax refund
- Selling stocks or bonds
- Mortgage equipment
- Returning merchandise
- Returning equipment
- Writing postdated checks

Or you could recommend that the owner just not pay someone else and pay you instead. This is a very effective idea that should not be overlooked.

If you are collecting from an individual, you could choose from the ideas listed previously or you could suggest that he get money from the following alternative sources:

- Advance from employer
- Odd jobs
- Bonus
- Vacation pay or sick pay
- Selling vacation days to another employee
- Second or part-time job
- Having spouse get a job
- Military reserve pay
- Pension
- Inheritance
- Garage sale
- Church
- IRA
- Hobby
- Selling or pawning car
- Pawning other items
- Unemployment check
- Welfare
- Social services
- Rebudget
- Recycle
- Christmas club
- Selling blood or plasma (Well, you never know.)

You and your debtor have the same objective. You both want the debt resolved. If your debtor pays, you both win. You get the money that is legally owed to you, and your debtor gets the satisfaction and relief of paying.

You might say to your debtor, "I can tell from talking with you that you are an honest person. I know you want to pay, don't you? I know that if you had the money in your pocket you would pay me. All we need to do now is find the money."

Let's see how this approach might work:

**You:** Your account is seriously delinquent, Mr. Smith, and must be paid now. Will you be in our office today or tomorrow to pay this account in full, or would you prefer to send us a check today for $200 so that we can clear this up?

**Debtor:** I just don't know what I'm going to do. My car broke down, and I had to pay to get it out of the shop. I just don't have any extra money right now.

**You:** Do you have any savings put away for an emergency like this?

**Debtor:** No, I just haven't been able to save any money.

**You:** Could you get an advance from your boss?

**Debtor:** No, my company has a strict policy against employee advances.

**You:** Do you have a life insurance policy that you could borrow from?

**Debtor:** No, I really wish that I had some life insurance.

**You:** Well, do you have any vacation days left at work?

**Debtor:** Yeah, I've got two weeks left—why?

**You:** Why don't you go to your boss and ask him if he will pay you for your vacation instead of you taking the time off?

**Debtor:** Hey, that's a great idea! We're really short of help at work and my boss may really like that idea.

This worked out nicely, didn't it? You and your debtor have worked together to come up with a mutually satisfactory solution. Now all you have to do is close the deal.

## Step 7, Close the Deal

It's important that you and your debtor agree to all the details of the proposed payment. You must review and reinforce your agreement and the more specific you are the better. You want to spell out exactly:

- how much the payment will be
- where the payment will be made
- when the payment will be made
- in what form the payment will be made

- Determine before you hang up the phone exactly how much the debtor is going to pay. Never allow the debtor to tell you that he or she will bring in as much as possible. Set an amount. Agree in advance.
- Determine exactly where the payment will be made. If the payment is to be made by mail, you will have to allow time for delivery. If the payment is to be made in person, you may have to give the debtor directions.
- Determine exactly when the payment is to be made. Always try to get the debtor to pay as soon as possible. Remember how important speed is in the collection process. The more time you give the debtor, the less chance you have of being paid.

If the debtor is going to come into your office, try to set an exact time for the appointment. This will give the debtor an urgent deadline and will let you know the minute that the debtor has broken his or her promise. If the debtor misses the appointment, you don't have to wait until the next day to follow up.

• Determine in what form the payment will be made. Is the payment going to be cash, check, money order, credit card, or draft?

Make your debtor think about and review the whole payment process in advance of payment. This reinforcement will increase your likelihood of payment.

Now let's work our example through to conclusion:

**You:** Why don't you go to your boss and ask him if he will pay you for your vacation instead of you taking the time off?

**Debtor:** Hey, that's a great idea! We're short of help at work and my boss may really like that idea.

**You:** Great! You can talk with your boss tomorrow morning and drop by our office during your lunch hour.

**Debtor:** I'll talk with him tomorrow, but it usually takes a day or two to get a check cut. I'll be in on Thursday.

**You:** You'll be in during lunch?

**Debtor:** I'll see you no later than 1 o'clock.

**You:** That's fine—I'll expect you [where] in our office [when] this Thursday by 1 o'clock with a payment of [how much] $200. We'll cash your [what form of payment] vacation check for you so that you won't have to stop by the bank.

**Debtor:** Thanks for working with me. I've had such a hard time and it will be such a relief to get this bill behind me.

Don't you wish everything in life were this easy?

## Step 8, Document Your Collection Effort

Hold it. You're not quite through yet. Enter into your computer or write on your account card or computer printout all the details of your collection call. This written information will come in handy if your debtor misses making the payment and could save you from a misunderstanding later.

# What to Do When You Have Limited Resources

*The efficiency expert walked up to the first worker and asked about his job responsibilities. The worker replied, "I don't do a thing." The expert then approached a second worker who also replied, "I don't do a thing." The expert exclaimed, "Aha, I've been here only two minutes and I've already found two employees doing the exact same job!"*
*—Anonymous*

## Take a Lesson from Lucy

You might consider skipping this chapter if you and your staff have ample time and resources to collect your delinquent accounts. But if you are unable to do a thorough collection job, then you need to pay close attention.

Whenever we see a company that's getting farther and farther behind in its collection work, we are reminded of a classic episode of *I Love Lucy*. In this episode Lucy and Ethel find a job in the wrapping department of a candy factory. Ethel originally had been given the task of boxing chocolates, but they kicked her out fast, because she "kept pinching the candy to see what kind they were."

Their supervisor gave them the following instructions: "Now the candy will pass by on this conveyor belt and continue into the next room where the girls will pack it. Now your job is to take each piece of candy and wrap it in one of these papers and then put it back on the belt."

Everything went well for a while, but soon the conveyor belt began moving faster and faster and Lucy and Ethel had difficulty keeping up. Ultimately the belt started moving so fast that it became impossible for them to wrap every piece of candy. They had to hide the surplus candy in their mouths, in their hats, down their dresses, or any place they could find.

We can easily make an analogy between what happens to an understaffed collection department in a growing business and what happened to Lucy and Ethel in the candy factory:

Conveyor belt = sales level
Candy = customers
Lucy and Ethel = collection department
Unwrapped candy = bad debts

When an entrepreneur writes a business plan, she assumes that her customers are going to pay as agreed and, for the most part, she is correct. But as her business grows, her delinquencies grow also. Soon her past due accounts increase to the point that she can't disregard them. But she doesn't want to utilize her limited resources to make customers pay their bills. She wants to invest in sales, marketing, technology—the things that make her business the biggest and the best.

But look what happens. As the conveyor belt (sales

level) moves faster and faster, the number of pieces of candy (customers) accelerates, and soon Lucy and Ethel (the collection department) can't get all their work done. The amount of unwrapped candy (bad debts) significantly increases and the business starts to suffer.

The company has the following alternatives:

- Slow down the conveyor belt (have fewer sales).
- Hire Fred, little Ricky, and the boys in the band to help (invest more resources in the collection effort).
- Have Lucy and Ethel continue to work at their maximum level with a lot of candy being left unwrapped (file away all delinquent accounts).
- Have Lucy and Ethel continue to work at their maximum level, but contract out the excess wrapping to a subcontractor (hire a collection agency to collect those accounts that are too difficult or time-consuming).

Having fewer sales is probably not acceptable, because most businesses would prefer not to cut sales or revenues. And we would be throwing money away if we filed away all our past due accounts. So our remaining options are to spend more on our collection effort or contract out.

There is no right decision that is true every time. Your objective should be to maximize profits. You must estimate your recoveries under each alternative and then compare the cost. Sometimes you'll be better off investing in your collection effort; other times you should contract out.

## Perform Triage

When you have too many accounts to collect, in addition to deciding *how* to handle them, you must also decide *which* ones to collect first.

When you have limited resources, always work your newest delinquencies first and leave your oldest delinquencies for last. It's human nature to want to try to collect your oldest accounts first. But, as we've discussed previously, as an account ages, the chances of collection drop rapidly. You don't want to waste your time and frustrate yourself trying to collect your most difficult accounts, when you could be successfully collecting your more current accounts and preventing future delinquencies. Collecting an old bill every once in a while may be an exhilarating experience and may make you feel really good about yourself, but if you've allowed five times as many problem accounts to develop in the meantime, you've made a costly mistake.

This may be easier to understand if we work through another analogy. Assume you are a doctor who has just moved to a small village in Africa. Unfortunately, the first week you begin your practice, there's an outbreak of a highly contagious and deadly plague that spreads savagely through the village's population. The plague is usually curable in its early stages, but as it progresses, the odds of recovery decrease significantly. You are the only doctor in the area and you don't have the time to physically treat everyone.

Do you spend all your time trying to save the terminally ill patients in the last stages of the disease, or do you try to treat the patients who have just gotten sick, knowing that your chances for success will be significantly higher? As a doctor and as a human being, it would be difficult for you to turn your back on the terminally ill, but being a rational person, you know you have no other choice. Your objective is to save the most lives. If you have limited resources, you have to prioritize.

If you were a football coach, would you line up your entire defense 50 yards back from the line of scrimmage to protect yourself from the long play, or would you concentrate your effort at the line of scrimmage? It's true, from time to time, the offense will break through for a big gain, but if you keep all your players back, your opponent will gain big every time.

As the credit manager, collection manager, or owner of a growing business, you can't afford to put all your efforts 50 yards back. You must concentrate your energies and resources near the line of scrimmage or you'll never stop your debtors. Instead of having one or two of your customers break through every once in a while, you'll have them all overrun you. If you have limited resources, you must not waste your time and efforts on the terminally ill. You will improve your collection results, cash flow, and profits if you put your company's resources into collecting your more current and, therefore, more collectible accounts.

Several years ago, we at Mr. King Furniture had a very successful advertising campaign. (Actually it may have been too successful.) We doubled our sales within a year. Our bad debts, however, quadrupled. We didn't have enough time or money to try to collect all of these accounts. Things were out of hand. We finally gained control when we gave up trying to collect the oldest accounts and put all our efforts into collecting the more current ones. We had the largest bad debt charge off in the history of the world, but the next month we were organized and back on our feet.

It can be a very difficult decision to give up collecting money that is legally and morally owed to you. But if your business is growing, your bad debts are escalating, and you are getting farther and farther behind, you can either upgrade your collection department or prioritize your collection effort.

Keep in mind that the objective of your business is to make a profit. Your objective is not to have zero bad debts.

You can often be more profitable with increased sales and
increased delinquencies than you would be with flat sales
and flat delinquencies.

At some point you must give up your collection effort.
Remember the law of diminishing returns. It makes no
sense to spend $1.50 to collect $1. And don't believe the
argument that if you allow one debtor not to pay that the
word will get around and no one will pay. This is just not
true.

And you certainly don't want to be guilty of trying to
collect your debt to get even with your debtor, or teach
him or her a lesson. You're trying to make money—not
teach morals or values.

So what do you do with those accounts that you aren't
able to collect yourself and you don't want to file away?
You can turn them over to an outside firm. But do you
litigate? These options are discussed in Chapter 16.

# What to Do When the Candy Gets By

QUESTION: What is black and brown and looks
good on an attorney?
ANSWER: A Doberman.

## Litigation

QUESTION: During the collection process when do
you hire an attorney to litigate?
ANSWER: After you have tried everything else.

There was a report on ABC-TV's *Good Morning America* that contrasted American and Japanese day-care centers. A video was shown of a day-care classroom in Japan. Next, a day-care facility in the United States was featured.

The Japanese classroom was in total chaos. A teacher was present, but her students appeared to be completely out of control. The teacher didn't seem to be supervising her students, and appeared to be oblivious to the anarchy.

The camera followed the antics of an unruly four-year-old boy. He picked on and bullied his classmates. He teased them. He pushed them. He stole their toys. But the teacher didn't seem to notice or care. The children had to fend for themselves.

On one occasion the little terror took a big whack at one of his fellow playmates. The teacher didn't even look up. Some children ran to her to complain, but she offered no help, and sent them back to play. After a while the children began avoiding this unruly child and he became a social outcast. Eventually the situation calmed down and things were resolved without the teacher's intervention.

The American day-care facility was quite different. Again we were shown a teacher with a classroom full of small children. And again there was one unmanageable child. But every time this brat picked on one of the other children, one of his playmates ran to the teacher for help and she came to the rescue. Toward the end of the video, the unruly child got into a serious fight. The teacher picked up the combatants and put one on each knee. She talked with them and resolved the conflict.

The differences between the two classrooms were startling. The children in the Japanese video were left to themselves and were expected to work out their own problems. The American children depended on their teacher to resolve their conflicts. The videos brought to light a major difference between two countries. The Japanese try to resolve conflict among themselves without third-party mediation, whereas Americans depend on the legal system to maintain order.

Instead of trying to work things out among ourselves, Americans tend to run to attorneys and judges. We are quick to choose legal intervention. In the United States there is one attorney for every 350 people. In Japan there is one attorney for every 10,000 people.

Frequently, litigation is not appropriate for debt collection. The balance of the debt may not be large enough to warrant the expense of a lawsuit or there may not be assets to attach or a job to garnishee. When a lawsuit is an option, it should be saved for last. The order of the collection process should be to (1) collect yourself, and if unsuccessful (2) turn over to a collection agency, and if unsuccessful (3) litigate.

Try to avoid litigation if possible. Legal action is the most drastic and most expensive form of collection. Remember that your objective is to collect the most money as fast as you can, net of expenses, while maintaining the goodwill of the debtor. By putting legal action ahead of other collection alternatives, you fail in every area. Don't pull out your big guns until the only option is a shoot-out.

• *Legal action can be expensive.* Many attorneys require an up-front noncontingency suit fee. This means that you pay the attorney a percentage of the debt whether or not it's collected. Even if the attorney agrees to collect on a contingency fee basis, you almost always have to pay court costs or filing fees when a lawsuit is filed. If the debt is not collected, this money is lost forever.

• *Legal action is not fast.* When you threaten someone with a lawsuit, a smart debtor will say, "Hot dog! I've just bought myself some additional time." Even if your lawsuit is successful, it can take a long time before the debt is recovered. Remember that time is the weapon of the debtor and the lawsuit process is long and tedious, proceeding along the lines of the following:

1. The debt is turned over to an attorney.
2. The lawsuit is filed.
3. The papers are served.
4. You wait for the debtor to answer and go to trial or you enter a default judgment.
5. You record the judgment.

6. Postjudgment remedies are executed (attach assets or wages).
7. Then, if you are lucky, the debt is collected.

In some states, after obtaining a judgment, you still aren't allowed to attach the debtor's wages. Many times creditors are surprised to learn that a recorded judgment against a debtor doesn't always collect the debt.

In the meantime the debtor could have:

- quit, been laid off, or lost his job
- moved or skipped
- gotten sick, been in an accident, or died
- filed for Chapter 7, 11, or 13 bankruptcy
- gotten divorced

To make our point using actual numbers, see Figure 5, which is a report that we generate each month for our retail furniture store. This report tells us how much we

Figure 5    Sample attorney placement and recovery report.

| Date | Placements ($) | Collections ($) | Percentage Recovered (%) |
|------|------|------|------|
| January | 22,900 | 2,173 | 9.49 |
| February | 16,488 | 0 | 0 |
| March | 7,706 | 0 | 0 |
| April | 13,606 | 0 | 0 |
| May | 2,387 | 0 | 0 |
| June | 11,680 | 0 | 0 |
| July | 16,963 | 0 | 0 |
| August | 7,949 | 0 | 0 |
| September | 5,802 | 0 | 0 |
| October | 6,395 | 0 | 0 |
| November | 16,798 | 0 | 0 |
| December | 7,963 | 0 | 0 |
| Total for Year | 136,637 | 2,173 | 1.59 |

collect through litigation for each month of placement. The first column indicates the month the accounts were sent to the attorney. The second column is the total balances turned over to the attorney plus all expenses of litigation. The third column shows how much we have collected for that specific month of placement. And the final column indicates the percentage of dollars that has been returned to us to date.

Twelve months after litigation, we recovered $2,173. However, we had advanced $2,567 in filing fees. Therefore, after one full year, we were $394 worse off than when we started. We will eventually recover money through litigation, but as you can see, it is not fast.

• *Legal action does not maintain the goodwill of the debtor.* When most prudent businesspeople receive a lawsuit or a threat of lawsuit from an attorney, they usually react by calling their own attorney. Since they didn't graduate from law school, they feel at a disadvantage in trying to negotiate with a licensed attorney on legal matters. So their direct communication with their creditor is cut off. Instead of two businesspeople talking with one another to work out their differences, you end up with two lawyers threatening one another (usually on an hourly basis).

Let's assume you go back to your office today and find a lawsuit on your desk. How might you react? You probably wouldn't feel a warm and close friendship to the party who is suing you. It's even possible that under the right circumstances, you might try to get even with a counterclaim. And once the dispute is resolved, it's doubtful you would want to do business with the plaintiff again.

Our agency handles a lot of medical collections. Doctors and medical administrators are very concerned about malpractice suits. Our agency, like many other professional agencies, tries to collect without suit when possible.

We don't want a patient to say, "If they're going to sue me, then I'll get myself an attorney and sue them."

Do you want to take action that might cause your debtor to run to his or her attorney? It only makes sense that the odds of a malpractice suit or counterclaim increase when a doctor sues a patient or a business sues its customer. Even if your debtor doesn't countersue, litigation effectively kills any chance of maintaining any type of relationship. Lawsuits should be evaluated on a case-by-case basis and used only when all else fails.

Try to collect the debt yourself first. If that doesn't work, consider turning your account over to a collection agency. If you are still unsuccessful, then the debt can always be litigated.

## Collection Agencies

Collection agencies understand that people who have fallen behind on their bills for reasons other than fraud need guidance. Agencies try to help these debtors settle their accounts without litigation. Choosing a collection agency, however, can sometimes be a challenge. At last count, by the American Collectors Assoc. (ACA), there are 7,400 collection agencies in the United States. Their quality and approach can vary widely. In many states all you have to do to open a collection agency is get a telephone.

How do you know which agency is best for you? You must do your homework. You want to ask for a client list and thoroughly check the references. If possible, try to tour the agency personally, meet the employees, and watch and listen to them in action. Your collection agency is an extension of your business. Everything they do and say reflects on you.

You should determine in advance specifically how

much collection effort you expect from your agency by having written work standards, and if you have enough volume to warrant the time, audit your agency to make sure it's doing the collection work that it promises. An agency that is doing its job won't mind. Then you'll want to ask a lot of questions:

- ☐ How long have you been in business?
- ☐ Who are the owners?
- ☐ Are you bonded?
- ☐ Do you keep your clients' monies in a separate trust account?
- ☐ Do you use the telephone or mail letters?
- ☐ Do you charge a contingency fee?
- ☐ How much is your fee?
- ☐ Are there any other charges?
- ☐ How do you collect small balances?
- ☐ Do you supply collection reports?
- ☐ What information is included in your reports?
- ☐ How often do you send reports?
- ☐ When are monies remitted?
- ☐ Do you deduct your fees or remit the full amount?
- ☐ Do you have any other clients like me?
- ☐ Who are your major clients?
- ☐ How many collectors do you have?
- ☐ What type of collector training do you have?
- ☐ How do you monitor your collectors?
- ☐ How do you handle disputes?
- ☐ What territories do you serve?
- ☐ What are your hours of operation?
- ☐ Are you computerized?
- ☐ How do you handle accounts that require suit?
- ☐ What credit-reporting agencies do you use?
- ☐ Do you belong to the Better Business Bureau?
- ☐ Do you belong to a professional association such as The

American Collectors Association or The International Association of Commercial Collectors?

If you have a large volume of accounts, you might consider splitting your collection work between two agencies to create a healthy competition. If you have a very large volume of accounts, you might select three or more agencies and then replace the worst performing agency every once in a while. Be sure to report results of your evaluation (see Chapter 17) to your agencies on a regular basis so they'll know how they're doing versus their competition. This will spur everyone to a higher level of performance and increase your recoveries.

After you select an agency, remember that you and the agency are both on the same team. If your personnel at your agency are successful, they will recover more money for you. Supply them with the information they need to do a good job. Answer their questions and when they require a response, get back to them as soon as possible. If you receive a payment, notify them, and if you find any new information on the debtor, let them know immediately.

Remember, top collection agencies hire professional, experienced collectors who are well trained and well supervised. They have collection tools available to them most businesses can't afford and are highly motivated to earn a commission. They are experts and specialists and they perform a task that most people would rather not do.

The best collection agencies are very labor-intensive and have high personnel costs. You want to allow your agency an opportunity to make a profit. If you cut its fees too low, it will be forced to reduce its effort. This will only hurt you. No agency is going to lose money on purpose.

Also remember that high recovery is not your only consideration. An unprofessional agency can be overzealous in its collection effort. This could result in unnecessary debtor complaints and additional problems for you. So you'll want to be sensitive to the type and number of complaints you receive and notify your agency at once if the number of complaints becomes unreasonable.

It is normal, however, to get an occasional debtor complaint. There will always be some debtors who want to avoid paying and will make frivolous accusations to avoid payment.

If you choose the proper agency and work together with its personnel as a team, you will collect the most money, as fast as you can, net of expenses, and still have the opportunity to maintain the goodwill of your debtors.

# How to Evaluate and Pay Outside Services

*Competition is so bad in our industry that we stab*
*each other in the front.*
*—Anonymous*

Many office managers, credit managers, or owners have no rational way of evaluating their collection agency or attorney. When asked, How good is your collection agency? the conversation often goes like this:

**Manager:** They seem to be doing a good job

**Sher:** How do you measure their results?

**Manager:** I get a nice check every month.

**Sher:** What percentage of the amount you turn over to them for collection do you recover?

**Manager:** I don't really know.

To be honest, we rarely have this conversation with a credit manager, because most of the time he doesn't know the recovery percentages. So he fabricates an answer or is just plain embarrassed. Since we are trying to build a business relationship with this individual, it is not in our best interest to belittle him. So the real conversation more than likely goes like this:

> **Sher:** How good are the people at your collection agency or your attorney?
>
> **Manager:** They are doing a good job.

What the manager's response generally means is "They are very nice," or "The owner's my brother-in-law," or "We've done business with them for years."

We're talking about cash flow here—real dollars. You would think that the credit manager would want some logical, businesslike way to evaluate how his agency or attorney is performing.

## Net Back

If you were to ask a real estate expert, "What are the three most important factors in evaluating real estate?" the answer would be "location, location, and location." If you were to ask a credit/collection professional "What are the three most important factors in evaluating outside collection services?" he or she would tell you "Net back, net back, and net back."

Recall that the first three objectives of optimal collections are to (1) collect the most money (2) as fast as you can (3) net of expenses. Your objective when choosing an outside collection service should be the same, particularly regarding "net of expenses," or net back. *Net back* is defined as the money that you get to keep, net of all fees and charges. (*You get to keep* are the key words here.)

There are drastic variations in the ways collection agencies and attorneys charge. Many charge a contingency fee, which is an agreed-upon percentage of the amount collected that the service provider earns for its work. The provider only earns a fee when it is successful in its collection. For instance, if the amount recovered is $100 and the contingency fee is 33 percent, then the provider earns $33. In our opinion, this is the most desirable way to compensate, because if the service provider doesn't produce, then you don't pay, and this is a real motivator for providers. If they collect nothing, then they earn nothing.

Some agencies charge a fixed amount per account—no matter how much or how little they collect. Letter services typically charge their clients a certain dollar amount per account to send out a series of letters. The letter service gets that dollar amount per account in advance no matter how high or low its recoveries.

Some collection attorneys charge a noncontingency suit fee. The creditor is required to advance a percentage of the balance turned over for collection whether or not any money is collected. If the balance referred to the attorney is $1,000 and the noncontingency fee is 10 percent, then the creditor pays a nonrefundable $100 cash payment to the attorney. If no money is recovered, then the creditor is out the $100. Then if the collection is successful, the attorney earns an additional contingency fee. For example, if there is a 15 percent contingency fee, the creditor pays another $150 in addition to the $100 already fronted.

Some attorneys, on the other hand, charge only for their time to draft a letter or call the debtor.

Some agencies and attorneys charge additional fees. There may be a service charge for listing accounts. There may be a charge for postage, copying, or skip tracing (trying to locate a lost debtor). Some collection attorneys charge administrative or trial fees. And of course, if litigation is required, you will incur court costs that you might not ever recover.

To compare one collection service with another, subtract all charges and fees from the total amount recovered and divide by the amount turned over for collection. This is your net back. All things being equal, the outside service that provides the largest dollar recovery percentage, net of expenses, will be your most profitable option.

Most professional collection agencies and attorneys will provide you with a report that calculates and discloses this information. If your collection firm can't or won't provide this report, then you need to compute it yourself. See Figure 6 for a sample. Accounts totaling $12,100 were turned over to this collection agency in the first four months of the year. An amount of $6,600 was recovered and there were $2,200 in commissions paid. Therefore, the creditor recouped $4,400 after fees. When you divide the $4,400 recovered (net of fees and expenses) by the $12,100 placed, you get a 36 percent net-back percentage. Remember to deduct all collection expenses, such as uncollected court costs or filing fees, against this net-back percentage.

This 36 percent figure can be used as a benchmark to compare how this agency does over time. If you have a large enough volume of accounts to warrant having one

Figure 6    Sample net-back calculation report.

| Month Account Placed | Amount Placed ($) | Amount Recovered ($) | Amount Recovered (%) | Commission (33¹/₃%) | Net Back to You ($) | Net Back (%) |
|---|---|---|---|---|---|---|
| January | 100 | 100 | 100 | 33 | 67 | 67 |
| February | 1,000 | 500 | 50 | 167 | 333 | 33 |
| March | 10,000 | 6,000 | 60 | 2,000 | 4,000 | 40 |
| April | 1,000 | 0 | 0 | 0 | 0 | 0 |
| Total | 12,100 | 6,600 | 55 | 2,200 | 4,400 | 36 |

or more agencies, you could use this 36 percent figure to evaluate the competition.

You'll want this comparison to be fair. You cannot give all the smaller balances to one agency; all the legally collectible accounts to another agency; and all the accounts that cannot be located to still another agency. And you must give your newest agency enough time to compete, because there's a learning curve and it may take it some time to maximize its results.

Even if you only use one agency or attorney, the net-back figure is still important. You want to review the net back on a regular basis to make sure your service provider is continuing to perform at a high level. Frequently the collection agency or attorney's recoveries drop over time and the client doesn't even notice.

This really happened. We were trying to sell a credit manager on the benefits of using our agency. We asked him the magic question: "How is your outside collection firm doing?" He responded, "Great!" We then asked if he would mind sharing with us its recovery percentages. He said that he didn't mind at all because it was recovering 100 percent.

We couldn't believe our ears because no agency or attorney ever recovers 100 percent on a long-term basis. So we asked him to explain. He said, without blinking an eye, "Of all the accounts that I have turned over for collection that had been paid in full, the recovery percentage was 100 percent." He was right.

Oh, by the way, you won't be surprised to learn that this credit manager is no longer employed at that company.

## Recovery Versus Fee

The percentage of dollars that your agency or attorney recovers is usually more important than the percentage contingency fee charged!

Most of the time you are better off paying a higher contingency fee and having a high recovery than paying a lower contingency fee and having a low recovery. Most people assume that the collection agency or attorney with the lowest contingency fee is their most profitable option and choose accordingly.

Let's see if that's true. Assume that $100 in bad debts are turned over to five different collection agencies on the same day. Now it's your choice. Refer to the chart shown as Figure 7. Would you prefer to do business with Agency A that only charges 10 percent and will give you back $9 for every $100 in placements, or would you rather do business with Agency E that charges an aggressive 50 percent and sends you a check for $25? Hopefully you'll choose the agency that brings you back the most money rather than the agency that simply charges you the lowest fees. Note in every row of the chart that the higher recovery percentage is worth more to you than the lower contingency fee.

Your first choice should be to choose the agency with the highest recoveries *and* the lowest contingency fees. But you don't want to negotiate a fee that's so low that you take away the incentive for the agency to invest enough time and resources to do a quality job. This will result in fewer recoveries and less money to you.

Figure 7   Recovery percentage versus contingency percentage.

| Agency | Amount Recovered (%) | Amount Recovered ($) | Contingency Fee (%) | Agency Keeps ($) | Net Back to You ($) |
|--------|----------------------|----------------------|---------------------|------------------|---------------------|
| A | 10 | 10 | 10 | 1 | 9 |
| B | 20 | 20 | 20 | 4 | 16 |
| C | 30 | 30 | 30 | 9 | 21 |
| D | 40 | 40 | 40 | 16 | 24 |
| E | 50 | 50 | 50 | 25 | 25 |

We're going to let you in on a little collection agency/ attorney secret. If you were to get competitive bids on like brands and models of cars, appliances, or even pencils with the same specifications, you would probably do well to purchase from the firm with the lowest price. However, a collection agency or attorney can charge you as low a contingency fee as you want and then cut back on their efforts in order to make a profit. If you want to pay a 20 percent contingency fee, then you can probably negotiate that rate. If you want to pay 10 percent, you might be able to negotiate that also. The agency or attorney won't be able to put much effort into collecting your accounts, but their contingency fee will certainly be dirt cheap.

Let's make the ridiculous assumption that you are clever enough to negotiate the contingency fee down to 0 percent. What a deal! We'll bet, however, that your agency won't put much effort into collecting your accounts since it has no economic incentive It won't collect anything and you'll get to keep 100 percent of nothing.

We're not saying that the amount of the contingency fee is not important—it is. But you want to allow your service provider an opportunity to earn enough to do a quality job.

Here's an example of what can happen to you when you negotiate a contingency fee that is too low. We convinced a large potential client to send us some accounts. He agreed to give us a chance, but asked for a lower contingency fee than we expected. We were uncomfortable with his request, but it became clear that if we didn't agree to his demands, we wouldn't get the business.

We didn't know it at the time, but the client didn't keep any records, so he didn't know how much we should recover. We had never collected this type of business before so we didn't know what to expect either. We went to work and felt like we were doing a good job. We asked the client and he seemed pleased also.

Then one day, we got an unexpected call from our client. He was coming for a surprise audit. A day after the audit, we got a call from the client. He was upset. He said that we were not doing the quantity and quality of work he had expected and told us to come by his office the next morning.

To be prepared for the meeting, we sat down with our collection manager to review the situation. It didn't take long to see the problem. Our computer prints a report each month showing the profit or loss for each client. We were losing money on this client and the manager cut back on the collection effort to stop the bleeding. The previous month, the manager had finally found the level of work at which we were no longer taking a loss.

The next day, we met with the client. He said that we weren't doing all the collection tasks he anticipated. We then showed him our profit analysis report and pointed out that we were losing money. We then asked a question that we should have asked at the beginning, "How come you quit using your previous agency?" He responded that the agency had been stealing from him.

We explained to him that with the small contingency fee he was willing to pay, an honest agency had only two options. The agency could either lose money or cut back on the collection effort in order not to lose money. It was certainly not acceptable for us to lose money, so we had to either raise our fee or work out a reasonable work standard. This would enable us an opportunity to make a profit and still satisfy him.

Both we and the client both learned a valuable lesson. The client now knows to negotiate a realistic level of work that is consistent with the fee negotiated. He also knows to spell out in advance the work standards required so the agency knows what is expected. In all fairness to our manager, there were no specific work requirements for him to follow, so in order to continue to do business with our client, he made decisions to prevent us from losing money.

Today, we are much more assertive and up front with potential clients now. If they request a fee that is too low to do a quality job, we tell them what level of work they can expect. They can then choose that level of work or accept a more realistic fee. It's true they may choose to do business with another agency, which may or may not be as honest with them, but we know we will never knowingly disappoint a client again.

# Make Collections
# Fun—Keep Score

*The big banner at Dell Computer Corp.'s plant in
Austin, Texas, read: "Glen will take a pie in the face for
2200 shipped in 10." Translation: To meet some big
orders, Dell Vice President Glenn Armbruster would let
workers slather him with whipped cream if they
produced 2,200 computers in ten hours. They did and
he was. A relatively small price to pay, he figured, to get
his point across.*
—Forbes, *June 6, 1994*

Prioritize the following list. Write the number 1 next to
the activity that you find the most desirable. Place a 2
next to the second most desirable, and so on.

- ☐ Take a Caribbean cruise.
- ☐ Eat at a nice restaurant.
- ☐ Take a few weeks off work to relax.
- ☐ Make collection calls.
- ☐ Win $1,000,000 in a lottery.

You probably rated "making collection calls" number 5. And our guess is that even if the list had been more realistic, you still would have selected "making collection calls" as one of your least desirable activities.

Many people who have collection responsibilities also have other duties. They always choose to do their other work first and save collections for last. They will open the mail, answer the phone, take out the trash, even offer to help their coworkers before they will pick up the telephone and make collection calls. You want everyone to treat your cash flow as a priority, but most people don't like to ask for money. The solution is to make collections fun. Collections don't have to be boring. Collections don't have to be monotonous. You can make your collection effort fun and exciting. All you need to do is set goals, measure your results, and create competition.

## Competition as Motivation

A number of years ago, volunteers were driven to a large warehouse-type building. Each was given a big black heavy ball with holes for their fingers. They were told that ten wooden pins had been placed at the end of a long passageway and they were asked to knock down as many of these pins as possible. But the pins were blocked from view by a large opaque curtain.

Each participant was then instructed to pick up his big black heavy ball, walk forward a few steps, lean over, and roll it down the alley. The ball quickly rolled out of sight behind the curtain. The ball then returned. Each volunteer picked up his ball again and repeated the process over and over. Pick up the heavy ball, walk forward, bend, and thrust. Pick up the heavy ball, walk forward, bend, and thrust. This was backbreaking work. This routine was definitely not fun, and soon each volunteer became bored and quit.

Thousands of people leave work every day and rush to their nearest bowling alley. They pick up their heavy ball, walk forward, bend, and thrust. They have a great time. When they knock over all the pins, they jump up and down and cheer with excitement. They can't wait to come back.

The volunteers we described were performing exactly the same activity, and they became bored and quit. What's the difference? The only difference is that our volunteers were not allowed to see how they were doing.

Let's examine the popular sport of football. In the fall of the year millions of fans rush to football stadiums all over the country to watch their favorite high school, college, or professional teams. What would happen if all the yard markers were erased and the scoreboards removed? Spectators would see a bunch of football players running back and forth up and down a grassy field blocking one another and knocking each other down. It's probable that after a few minutes, even the most ardent football enthusiast would become disinterested and bolt for the exits.

If you were to remove "the keeping score" part from any sport, you would kill all interest in it. This would be true for baseball, basketball, gymnastics, or track. It's also true for collections.

Just turn collections into a sport—into a competition, and let your collectors see how they are doing. By measuring results and keeping score, your collectors will have fun. The worst thing you can do is to give someone accounts to collect and not let her know how she is doing. It would be just like going bowling with the pins hidden behind a curtain.

When it comes to collections, how do you create competition? What do you measure?

If you have two or more collectors, it's easy to create competition. Add a few prizes and you can really get everyone's adrenaline flowing. The prizes don't have to be expensive. Our collection manager, for instance, makes a paper crown out of discarded computer paper and places it on the head of the leading collector. The other collectors work like crazy to capture this ceremonial paper headdress.

We don't agree with negative rewards, but we once visited a collection department that used a similar idea in reverse. The collection manager made a dunce cap and placed it on the desk of the worst-performing collector.

You can offer prizes such as free lunches, ribbons, pins, or plaques. One collection supervisor told us that she agreed to shine the shoes of her leading collector and another promised to wash the car of any collector who met certain agreed-upon goals.

If you have a larger budget, you can increase the stakes for your collectors by offering them cash bonuses or more valuable prizes. You'll probably want to set minimum performance levels for major prizes to ensure that your collectors earn enough extra profit for your business to pay for these prizes. You could offer a cruise or a trip to the beach or mountains. A new TV, a VCR, or a CD player might be motivational. Prizes, both large and small, are only limited by your imagination.

Some collection managers prefer not to have their collectors compete against one another. They encourage teamwork with company or department goals and objectives. But all competition, whether individual against individual, or companywide goals, should be win–win. You achieve your collection goals—you win. Your collectors achieve their collection goals—they win.

Even if you have only one collector, you can make the collection work more interesting and keep him or her motivated. Just compare this month's collections to last month, last year, or to an agreed-upon goal. Post the results each day and watch as your collector "dials for dollars" and has a good time doing it.

We recommend, if possible, that you have your employees participate in the goal-setting process. Make sure that your goals require some stretch, but remain realistic. If you set a goal that's unreasonable, your collectors will give up before the contest begins.

## What Do You Measure and Reward?

What results do you reward? You might pay for increased collections or for decreased days outstanding. Or you might reward for reduced delinquencies. Try to avoid long contest periods so collectors don't lose interest. And be sure to reward collectors for small incremental improvements to sustain motivation over time.

At Mr. King Furniture we use three different reports to create competition and reward our collectors. One report shows the number of definite payment commitments for each collector for each hour worked. See Figure 8 as a sample. The left-hand column lists four collectors. The adjacent columns show how many promises each collector has gotten each hour, with daily totals listed in the right-hand column and hourly totals across the bottom.

Calling accounts is like going fishing. The more times you throw your bait into the water, the better your chances of catching a fish. The collector who gets the most promises will most likely get the most payments. That's assuming, of course, that his or her collection technique is also effective.

We use the report shown as Figure 9 to tabulate the effectiveness of each collector. Making a large quantity of

Figure 8   Sample of a report showing collectors' counts by hour of promises to pay obtained.

| Collectors | 9:00–10:00 | 10:00–11:00 | 11:00–12:00 | 12:00–1:00 | 1:00–2:00 | 2:00–3:00 | 3:00–4:00 | 4:00–5:00 | Daily Totals |
|---|---|---|---|---|---|---|---|---|---|
| Linda | 6 | 7 | 5 | 0 | 4 | 4 | 3 | 10 | 39 |
| John | 7 | 6 | 6 | 0 | 2 | 5 | 4 | 8 | 38 |
| Jerry | 8 | 5 | 3 | 1 | 3 | 1 | 3 | 4 | 28 |
| Mary | 5 | 3 | 4 | 1 | 3 | 0 | 4 | 5 | 25 |
| Hourly Total | 26 | 21 | 18 | 2 | 12 | 10 | 14 | 27 | 130 |

Figure 9   Report for tabulating collector effectiveness on a monthly basis.

| Name | Promises (month to date) | Successful | Percentage Successful (%) | Average Days Out |
|------|--------------------------|------------|---------------------------|------------------|
| John | 972 | 280 | 28.8 | 2 |
| Linda | 927 | 255 | 27.5 | 3 |
| Mary | 887 | 221 | 24.9 | 4 |
| Jerry | 883 | 212 | 24.0 | 5 |
| Total | 3,669 | 968 | 26.4 | 3.5 |

calls is important, but the *quality* of the call is important, too. The collector must say the right thing in the right way to persuade the debtor to pay.

In the report, the collectors' names are listed on the left. As you move to the right, you see how many promises have become due so far this month. The third column shows how many debtors actually made full payments on or before the promised due date, and the fourth column indicates what percentage of the time the collector was successful in collecting the payment.

Notice, on this report, that only 26 percent of the debtors actually paid after making a promise. This is an important statistic. It points out to our collectors that the odds of payment are only about one in four. This helps them deal with failure and rejection. They know they can expect to fail to receive payment on three out of every four promises. Also it is an important reminder to them that they have to make a lot of calls because 74 percent of the time their debtors aren't going to pay.

Look at the last column of Figure 9. This column, labeled "Average Days Out," indicates how many days on average each collector allowed each debtor to promise to pay. Generally speaking, the longer the collector gives the debtor, the worse the results will be. Note that John, the most effective collector, took promises for an average of two days. Jerry was the least effective collector. He gave his debtors five days.

Inexperienced collectors think they can increase their effectiveness percentages by giving their debtors extra time. They believe that if they allow more days to pay, the chances of receiving payment improve. As explained in Section Two, the opposite is actually true. The longer you give your debtors to pay, the less urgent it becomes to them. You want your debtors to have to deal with you now. Your debtors probably owe other people in addition to you, and if you give them extra time, their other creditors will call. Your debtors will then concentrate on paying them and worry about you some other time.

You can utilize the promise to pay by hour and effectiveness reports to train your collectors and help them do a better job. If a collector is not bringing in enough money, he or she either is not getting enough promises or is not saying the right thing. An analysis of these reports will point out the problem.

Finally, Figure 10 shows a report that measures cash collection by collector and therefore it is our most important report. The other two reports only measure activity. We pay our collectors cash incentives based on cash collections—not on activity.

As in the previous reports, the collector's name is

Figure 10    Collector incentive report.

| Name | Potential ($) | Collections (month to date) ($) | Percentage Successful (%) |
|------|---------------|---------------------------------|---------------------------|
| Linda | 56,198 | 47,656 | 84.8 |
| John | 53,645 | 43,667 | 81.4 |
| Mary | 54,116 | 43,687 | 80.7 |
| Jerry | 51,379 | 41,323 | 80.4 |
| Total | 215,338 | 176,333 | 81.9 |

listed on the left. Moving to the right, the column labeled "Potential" is the total amount of money that would be collected if every debtor made a full monthly payment during the month. The "Collections (month to date)" column indicates how much money has actually been collected to date, and the last column shows what percentage of the total has been collected so far.

Be careful that your incentive system is not manipulated by your employees. At a seminar presented by George Odiorne, who wrote the book *Management by Objectives,* he explained how the city of New York attempted to improve the productivity of its employees at a city landfill. It seemed that too much garbage was accumulating and something had to be done to speed up the processing.

A consultant suggested that the city pay cash incentives to the landfill workers if they achieved a certain level of productivity. He determined the best way to measure productivity was to weigh the amount of garbage processed.

Sure enough, the total weight of garbage processed increased dramatically and the workers began earning cash bonuses. But something was wrong. The garbage continued to pile up.

An inspector was sent to the landfill to investigate and it didn't take him long to determine what was wrong. The workers were wetting down the garbage before they weighed it, resulting in grossly exaggerated weight.

When you set up an incentive program or contest, you must watch your employees' behavior closely. Employees, on occasion, strive to make their figures look good rather than make the right decisions for your business.

## Are You Having Fun Yet?

Tom Peters, business guru and author, tells a story about Sam Walton, the founder of Wal-Mart Corporation. When

Mr. Walton was almost seventy years old, he promised his employees, "If they would give him an 8 percent pretax return, which is one heck of a return in the discount retailing business, that he would do the hoola on Wall Street in February." They did, and he did.

We could all increase cash flow dramatically if we would be as creative as Sam Walton.

Now take just a moment to prioritize one more list. Review the activities listed below and write the number 1 next to the activity that you find the most appealing. Then place a 2 next to the second most appealing activity, and so on.

☐ Go to the dentist to have a tooth drilled.
☐ Walk across a bed of hot coals.
☐ Have your brother-in-law, sister-in-law, and three kids move in with you.
☐ Make collection calls.
☐ Swim the English Channel with an anchor tied around your neck.

Who would believe it? After just a few minutes of reading, collection calls have jumped to the top of your wish list!

# A FEW FINAL
# WORDS

*A girl and her boyfriend were passing by a jewelry shop
and she said, "Oh, honey, if I had that diamond brooch
in the window I'd be the happiest girl in the world." So
he reached into his pocket, took out a brick, threw it
through the window, took the brooch, and gave it to her.
Continuing their walk, they came upon a furrier's with
a mink coat in the window, and she said, "Oh, honey, if
I had that mink coat I would be the happiest girl in the
world." Again he reached into his pocket, took out
another brick, threw it through the window, took the
coat, put it around her, and they walked on. Finally they
came to a Rolls-Royce dealer with a Silver Cloud Rolls
in the window, and she said, "Oh, honey, with the
brooch, the coat, and that car, I would be the happiest
girl in the world." He said, "Hey, do you think
I'm made of bricks?"*

## A Word About Avoiding All Bad Debts

Several years ago, David attended a speed-reading course at a local university. During the first class, the teacher asked a simple question that he and his classmates thought was absolutely absurd at the time. She asked, "Do you want to know how to read a book at the speed of one million words per minute?"

Naturally everyone in the class couldn't wait to hear the answer. They were disappointed, however, with her response of "Don't read the book." Her answer sounded ridiculous at the time, but after a class or two, they began to understand what she meant. She was simply saying be more selective about what they read. If they examine a book and determine that it's of little or no value, then they could save a lot of time by not reading it.

The same logic could be made about avoiding bad debts. Do you want to know how to have zero delinquencies and no bad debts? Don't sell your product or service on credit. Require cash in advance. For example, David tells about one time our mother phoned and said she wasn't feeling well. She asked him to take her to the doctor's office. The doctor examined her and requested she come back the following week. Upon leaving the examining room, our mother went directly to the receptionist to settle her account and make her follow-up appointment. The receptionist told her that it was the policy of the doctor's office to require payment in full at the time of service, but since she was coming back the following week, she could pay for both visits then.

Our mother had her hand in her purse ready to pay, but immediately withdrew it at the receptionist's suggestion of delayed payment. The receptionist could have avoided this accounts receivable altogether. Who knows what might happen by next week. Maybe our mom would feel better and not come back. Maybe she would be so ill she would have to miss the appointment. Maybe dear old Mom is a deadbeat who doesn't pay her bills.

The point is that the more money you get up front, the fewer bad debt you will ultimately have. So if you can require your customer to pay in advance, you will be way ahead.

## A Word About Consumer Collections

### Why Consumers Don't Pay

It's estimated by the American Collectors Association that 2 percent of all debtors are credit criminals (deadbeats who have no intention of paying). So why are delinquencies for most businesses worse than 2 percent? Many well-intentioned people don't do financial planning or if they do plan, they run into unexpected problems. They may default on their debts for any one or combination of the following reasons:

- Overobligation
- Marital problems (divorce or separation)
- Personal or family medical problems
- Reduced income (unemployment or fewer hours)

• Overobligation. Most people are not accountants and don't have an inclination or interest in budgeting. They don't sit down and figure out in advance whether they can afford their monthly payments. When they do budget, they don't take into consideration all of their expenses or consider all the things that can go wrong.

Here's a typical situation: Everything's going along

fine with Mr. and Mrs. Velasquez. All the bills are getting paid and there are even a few dollars a month left over to put in the bank. Then one day, Mrs. Velasquez looks up and sees a dark spot on the ceiling of the house. Mr. Velasquez has to hire a roofing company to put on a new roof. After the roofing company is paid, there is not enough money left over to pay the rest of the bills.

• Marital Problems. There are approximately 1.2 million divorces in the United States every year. That's 1.2 million couples who find their household income radically changed.

Here's a typical situation: Mr. and Mrs. Pettigrew both have good jobs. They buy a house and a car, and make other bills to build a life together. Then Mr. Pettigrew becomes dissatisfied. He says she's spending him out of house and home. She says he wastes all his time watching football. He finds a girlfriend. She finds an attorney. Then the attorneys make all the money and the court has to settle their differences. You call to collect a debt and she says he's responsible. You call him and he says she's responsible.

• Personal or Family Medical Problems. No one ever knows when they are going to get sick or injured and, unfortunately, many people aren't prepared.

Here's a typical situation: Mr. and Mrs. Horton are both working. She has a baby. The baby gets sick. He breaks a leg. He's out of work. The bills don't get paid.

• Reduced Income. Here's a typical situation: Mr. and Mrs. Digiorno are both drawing big paychecks. They earn more money every year and anticipate that things will only get better. Suddenly there's a cutback at the plant. He loses his job. Her hours are reduced. Now they can't pay all the bills.

## The Kitchen-Basket Syndrome

Most people intend to pay their bills. But most people are not "made of bricks," so they have to decide which bills to pay and which ones to put aside. Typically, they take their bills as they arrive and throw them in a basket in the kitchen. Then at the end of the month, they stack them in a pile and pay them in the following order:

1. House payment
2. Utility bills
3. Car payment
4. Bank credit cards
5. Department stores, doctors, dentists, and anyone else

At some point they run out of money before they run out of bills. If you are a creditor whose invoice is placed at the bottom of the stack, how do you get paid?

You persistently and consistently *ask* for your money. You let your debtor know that you are *not* going to be ignored. You make it clear that you are going to stick with them until they alter their usual order of payment.

## A Word About Commercial Collections

People often say to us, "Most of my customers/clients pay their bills, they just pay slowly. What should I do?" The most important thing you can do is emphasize to your customers the importance of prompt payment at the time of sale. Then if a payment is late, immediately call the customer. But in larger companies, you may not know whom to call. We therefore suggest that before any money is due, you get to know the person in your customer's organization who pays the bills. If that individual lives in your city, invite him or her to lunch and get acquainted. If that individual lives in another city, call him or her and build a relationship. Then, if the firm doesn't pay as agreed, you know who to call.

Your objective in commercial collections is the same as in consumer collections: to convince your debtor that he or she is better off paying than not paying.

One of the most creative commercial collection stories we have ever heard was told by a business owner at a Chamber of Commerce reception. When he heard that we were in the collection business, he couldn't wait to tell how he had collected from one of his clients.

He owns a communications business that sells to banks. A bank owed him $25,000 and he just couldn't seem to get it to pay. So he drove down to the main branch of the bank that owed him the money and asked to see a commercial loan officer. He told the banker that he wanted to borrow some money, but he had ample collateral to cover the loan. He said he wanted to use the accounts receivable owed by the bank as collateral. Within two hours of returning to his office, a courier brought him a check for the full $25,000.

## The Final Word—Lessons in Real Life

To wrap up our coverage of debt collection, David relates the following personal anecdote:

> Several months ago, my wife said those dreaded words, "Honey, you know the house is beginning to look a little run down, and I think it's time to have it redecorated." I said, "It's okay with me—as long as you handle everything." She hired a contractor to paint, put up new wallpaper, and lay carpet. His crew was to begin work the first of September.
>
> Sure enough on September 1, two of his finest men came to our comfortable, well-organized

home and began to disassemble it. Then after everything was in total disarray, they disappeared.

My wife called Bill, the contractor, and asked what had happened. He apologized and said that he had run into some problems on his "other job," but please don't worry because his men would be back in a week and pick up where they had left off. I'm not really sure, but I think my wife was contemplating homicide.

The week went by and no men showed up. My wife called back and Bill begged for another week. When that week passed, he asked for still another extension.

Not to worry. My wife was going to call in the cavalry—me.

She said, "Honey, would you please call an attorney and sue Bill?" I didn't want to have anything to do with this. After all this was her idea. She had promised me that she would handle everything. I didn't know what her remodeling plans were. I didn't know what promises the contractor had made. I wasn't going to get involved. . . .

Rather than sue him, I decided to call Bill myself. I asked him if he would sit down face-to-face with me and try to work out a solution. He met me at my office and explained that he had run into some personnel problems and was short of help. His other job had turned out to be much more difficult than he had anticipated. He promised that he had good intentions, but he couldn't leave his other job until he had completed it.

I judged that he was telling the truth, that he meant well, and that there was very little I could do about it. He was just a small contractor who had bitten off more than he could chew. Unfortunately, my wife had paid him too much money in advance and I didn't want to pay twice to have our home redecorated. So I asked him to please straighten up our house in the meantime and to give us a firm date of completion. He cleaned up our house as I had requested and he promised that he would be back full-time by November 15.

I called him about a week before his commitment date to make sure he was coming. He said that he was not quite finished with his other job and he needed another few days. I pinned him down to November 22 and called him the day before. He said he was running on schedule and would see me the next day. Believe it or not, the next day he and his men still did not show up. So I called him again. That day was Thursday and he explained that he had completed his other job, but his men were worn out and wanted to take a few days off before going back to work. He gave me his word that he and his crew would be back to our house first thing Monday morning.

He and his men came Monday morning as promised and our house was completely redecorated within a few weeks.

Now what does this story have to do with collections? Let's review it and you will see the parallels.

When my wife asked me to get involved, I had to determine my objective. (My objective actually was to avoid becoming one of the 1.2 million divorces forecast for the year.) I figured that I would accomplish my goal if I got our house decorated as fast as possible at the lowest possible cost while maintaining the goodwill of the contractor. After all, who wants to have an angry vindictive contractor working in their home? So my objective was roughly the same as that for optimal debt collection:

- To collect the most money . . . to get my house redecorated
- As fast as possible . . . as fast as possible
- Net of expenses . . . at the lowest possible cost
- While maintaining the goodwill of the debtor . . . while maintaining the goodwill of the contractor

If my wife had managed her redecorating project the way a good business receivable should be managed, then she might have avoided her contractor problems. My wife introduced me to the contractor after he had become the equivalent of a "delinquent account." She should have taken the first three steps of our walk down the "avenue":

Application: She should have gotten some references.
Verification: She should have called his references to determine the quality and timeliness of his work.
Expectations: She should have emphasized her expectations of completion date.

I believe, in all modesty, that I was able to get the decorating completed by the original contractor without additional expense because I followed good, sound collection techniques. It's true that it

was a lot of work. I had to ask and then ask again.
I had to be consistent and persistent. I had to re-
mind him before his commitment date, and when
he didn't show up, I had to call him back. I kept
the pressure on. I never raised my voice, but he
knew that I was not going away.

These are the same principles you want to follow
when you manage and collect your accounts receivable.

Collecting accounts is not just writing letters and making telephone calls. It is the way you run your business. It
begins the moment you or your employees first talk with
your customers. If you do all the little things right all
along, then you will have few collection problems later.
Never lose sight of the debt-collection objective we
have set out herein, and always *ask* for your money.

# Index